D0054335

The Ruler's Guide

*China's Greatest Emperor
and His Timeless Secrets of Success*

CHINGHUA TANG

SCRIBNER

New York   London   Toronto   Sydney   New Delhi

SCRIBNER

An Imprint of Simon & Schuster, Inc.

1230 Avenue of the Americas

New York, NY 10020

First Scribner hardcover edition February 2017

SCRIBNER and design are registered trademarks of The Gale Group, Inc., used under license by Simon & Schuster, Inc., the publisher of this work.

For information about special discounts for bulk purchases, please contact Simon & Schuster Special Sales at 1-866-506-1949 or business@simonandschuster.com.

The Simon & Schuster Speakers Bureau can bring authors to your live event. For more information or to book an event, contact the Simon & Schuster Speakers Bureau at 1-866-248-3049 or visit our website at www.simonspeakers.com.

Interior design by Kyle Kabel

Manufactured in the United States of America

1   3   5   7   9   10   8   6   4   2

Library of Congress Control Number: 2016011914

ISBN 978-1-5011-3877-5
ISBN 978-1-5011-3878-2 (ebook)

To my beloved parents,
QINGAN TANG *and* EILEEN H. GE,
who have dedicated their lives to teaching
and who have fostered in me a habit of reading.

Contents

vii

Contents

The Ruler's Guide

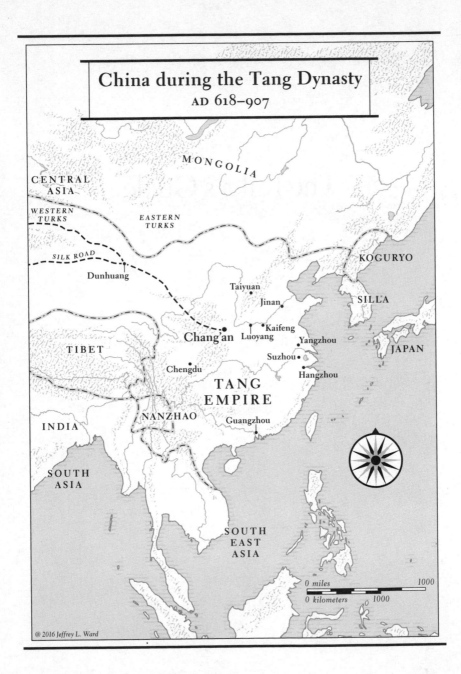

China during the Tang Dynasty
AD 618–907

MONGOLIA

CENTRAL ASIA

WESTERN TURKS

EASTERN TURKS

SILK ROAD

Dunhuang

KOGURYO

Taiyuan

Jinan

SILL'A

Kaifeng
Chang'an Luoyang
Yangzhou

TIBET

Suzhou

JAPAN

Chengdu

Hangzhou

TANG EMPIRE

NANZHAO Guangzhou

INDIA

SOUTH ASIA

SOUTH EAST ASIA

0 miles   1000
0 kilometers   1000

@ 2016 Jeffrey L. Ward

Introduction

The Tang dynasty, one of the longest dynasties in Chinese history (618–907), is hailed by historians as China's golden age. It didn't come about by chance. It owed much to the conscious efforts of its co-founder, Emperor Taizong.

Tang Taizong* is one of history's greatest rulers, ranking with Augustus, Genghis Khan, and Napoléon — and even, in some cases, exceeding their accomplishments. Under Taizong's leadership, China became the world's largest and strongest country. The emperor's reign was marked by a number of savvy, innovative, and bold accomplishments, setting a high standard for all leaders who would come after. Among the feats that make Taizong extraordinary:

- He assembled a team of advisers even *before* he assumed the throne at the age of twenty-eight.
- He was a gifted administrator, presiding over all major policy and executive decision-making at his court.

---

* Tang Taizong (598–649): "Tang" is the name of the dynasty and "Taizong" his imperial title as emperor. His personal name is Li Shimin.

1

- He was a master military strategist, leading his armies to defeat the Turks—descendants of Attila the Hun—and reopening the Silk Road.
- He slew a thousand enemy fighters by his own hand.
- He was remarkably versatile: an archer, hunter, horseman, poet, composer, and calligrapher.
- He allowed both Christianity and Islam into China for the first time and was, indirectly, the cause of Buddhism's being planted in Tibet.
- He was apparently expert at picking a wife: his empress was one of the wisest and most virtuous women in history.
- He set out to build a strong, prosperous, and long-lasting empire and succeeded spectacularly.

Tang Taizong and his circle of gifted ministers held many discussions regarding how best to run the government and achieve longevity for the dynasty. Most of their conversations were recorded and later compiled in an anthology entitled *The Zhenguan Executive Guide*. This book has since become a classic on leadership, management, and statecraft. It has been translated into Korean, Japanese, Mongolian, Khitan, Jurchen, and Tangut. It was eagerly read by rulers of China and other Asian countries—potentates such as the Mongol conqueror Kublai Khan, the Japanese shogun Tokugawa, and the Qing emperor Qianlong. Today, Taizong's thinking is ardently studied by business executives and government leaders throughout Asia. And it is far past time that the emperor's thoughts be shared with those in other parts of the world.

Wittingly or unwittingly, today's leaders—regardless of what organization they head—often assume the role of "ruler." Politically, the emperor is a thing of the past. However, an elected leader in many cases enjoys much the same power as an emperor within his or her domain. And, of course, business leaders and corporate managers are rulers in *their* world. There are rulers in virtually every field. For example:

The president of a trade union is the ruler of his[*] organization.

The head of a philanthropy is the ruler of his institution.

The headmaster is the ruler of his school.

The teacher is the ruler of his class.

The coach is the ruler of his sports team.

The conductor is the ruler of his orchestra.

The lieutenant is the ruler of his platoon.

The priest is the ruler of his local church.

Parents are the rulers of their family.

The list goes on and on. You may be a ruler in one situation and ruled in another. You may be ruler and ruled simultaneously. You may be ruled and yet aspire to be *the* ruler.

Whether running a country or a commercial enterprise, whether leading a team or serving as a role model, rulers

---

[*] The author recognizes the role of women in all spheres of modern life and asks the reader to make allowance for the use of masculine pronouns in the book.

wield enormous power over the people and the resources they command. They're capable of exerting great influence over the society, environment, and community in which they operate. And they face many problems that are similar to those an ancient emperor would have faced.

Many books have been written on leadership and management. This one is distinctive in that it is not a one-way stream of advice but, rather, an anthology of conversations between Tang Taizong and his ministers. And because the longevity of the Tang dynasty has always been considered proof of Taizong's wisdom, the principles disclosed here have stood the test of time.

A guide to enlightened conduct for *anyone* in a position of authority, *The Ruler's Guide* offers insight into many present-day management issues:

- How to attain self-knowledge
- How to evaluate people
- How to handle the relationship between moral character and talent
- How to exercise leadership
- How to enhance organizational effectiveness
- How to apply the art of war
- How to achieve long-term success

This book brings Taizong's wisdom to a Western audience for the first time—wisdom that has been studied and proven for more than a thousand years. In the pages that follow, records of the emperor's conversations with his ministers are selected and organized under twelve topics. They represent the choicest part of this anthology. Following that is a profile that sketches Taizong's extraordinary life and character. In the secrets of the Tang dynasty's success, you'll find the secrets of all great, long-lasting enterprises.

Since my family name is, coincidentally, the same as the dynasty that Taizong helped found, I take extra pleasure in bringing his wisdom to you.

I

CONVERSATIONS BETWEEN
TANG TAIZONG AND HIS MINISTERS

君臣对话

On Being Emperor

A great person attracts great people and knows
how to hold them together.

—GOETHE*

Taizong became emperor when he was twenty-eight years
old. His life began a new phase. He applied himself dili-
gently to learning the job.

Prompted partly by his need for help in governing the
country and partly by his desire to be an effective ruler,
he surrounded himself with a group of wise and dedicated
advisers from different backgrounds. He had many scintil-
lating conversations with them. He was a good listener, a
humble student, an eager learner, and a keen observer. He'd
proven his prowess in war. Now he set out to demonstrate
his ability to run a country.

* Johann Wolfgang von Goethe (1749–1832) was a German poet, writer,
scientist, and statesman, and is regarded as the greatest German literary
figure of the modern era.

TANG TAIZONG AND HIS ADVISERS' WORDS

THE RULER'S HEART

Early in his reign, Taizong told his ministers: "The ruler has only one heart, but it is the goal of many people. Some want to win it by bravery, some want to win it by eloquence, some by flattery, some by cunning, some by satisfying its desires. The ruler is being assaulted from all sides. Everybody tries to sell him something in order to attain power and wealth. If he drops his guard for one moment, he can make a serious mistake and get into trouble. That is why it is difficult to be a ruler."

BOW AND WOOD

Shortly after he ascended the throne, Taizong said to Minister Xiao Yu, "I have been fond of archery since I was a boy. I thought I knew everything about bows. A few days ago I received a dozen bows. When I showed them to a bow maker, he told me they were not good bows. I asked why. He said, 'Because the heart of the wood is not straight, so the veins are slanted. Although the bows are strong, they cannot shoot straight.'

"Then I realized even though I've been using bows for so many years I really don't know their secret. I must know even less about governing a country."

This realization prompted him to not only hold daily meetings with cabinet ministers but reach out frequently to junior officials as well in order to learn more about what was going on in the country.

STANDING UPRIGHT

Taizong said, "The ruler must conduct himself properly. If he stands straight, his shadow can't be crooked. If those above set a good example, those below will follow. In my opinion, what destroys the ruler is not something external. It is something internal. Unchecked desires will do harm to his body and mind; self-indulgence will interfere with his work. Then if he says something wrong, he will lose the support of the people completely."

"Exactly," responded Minister Wei Zheng. "Therefore sage kings of the past started with self-cultivation to try to nurture their virtues and overcome their weaknesses. This process enabled them to gain insight into many things and helped them to do a good job."

SELF-AWARENESS

Taizong said, "An enlightened ruler knows his own inadequacies, so he becomes wiser. A fatuous ruler tries to cover up his own faults, so he remains in a poor light."

HEAD AND BODY

In a memorandum to Taizong, Minister Wei Zheng wrote, "The ruler is the head and his ministers are the arms and legs. When they work with one mind and one heart, they become one body. The body cannot be whole if any part of it is missing. The head occupies the highest place, but it needs the arms and legs to form a complete body. The ruler may be wise, but he needs his ministers to help him govern the country."

BEFORE YOU SPEAK

Du Zhenglun was the court historian, whose job it was to write down everything the emperor said and did.

Taizong said to him, "Before I say anything at my daily audience, I'll think about how people may react to my words."

Du Zhenglun replied, "Your Majesty's words will not only have an impact here and now; they will be reflected upon by future generations too."

Taizong continued, "If an ordinary man says something wrong, it could bring shame on him. If the ruler has a slip of the tongue, the consequences could be disastrous. I will always keep that in mind."

APPROPRIATE MODESTY

Taizong consulted the renowned Confucian scholar Kong Yingda. "*Analects* says: 'Those who have talent should learn from those who do not. Those who are knowledgeable should learn from those who are not. If you are talented, act as though you are not. If you are knowledgeable, act as though you are not.' What does that mean?"*

"It means you should be modest," Kong Yingda answered, "so that you can accomplish great things. No matter how talented you are, you can enhance your talent further. No matter how knowledgeable you are, you can still expand your knowledge. The ruler should not show off his smartness. On the contrary, he should hide it. He should listen to others' good advice and not try to cover up his own mistakes. Otherwise, he will block communication with his subordinates and alienate himself from them. And that will bring him no good."

"Yes indeed," agreed Taizong. "The *Book of Changes* says, 'Blessed is he who is always humble.'"

HUMILITY

King Shun and King Yu are legendary sage rulers of China, who lived about four thousand years ago. Taizong looked up to them as his role models.

He said, "They say the Son of Heaven is all power and glory, with nothing to be afraid of. I disagree. Precisely

---

* *Analects* is one of the four authoritative books on Confucianism. The other three are *Great Learning, Doctrine of the Mean*, and *Mencius*. These four plus the five classics—*Book of Changes, Book of Songs, Book of Documents, Book of Rites*, and *Spring and Autumn Annals*—make up the Confucian canon.

because I am the Son of Heaven, I must be humble and fearful. As King Shun admonished his successor, King Yu, 'As long as you don't regard yourself as glorious, nobody can compete with you; as long as you don't consider yourself as great, nobody can defeat you.' Heaven favors humility and frowns upon pride. Whatever I say or do, I am mindful of Heaven and mindful of my subjects. Heaven sees everything; how can I not be fearful? My subjects look at me all the time; how can I not be careful? What I am concerned about is that my deed and my word may not find favor in their sight."

Minister Wei Zheng responded, "As the saying goes, 'There are many good beginnings, but few good endings.' It is my hope that Your Majesty will always be humble, fearful, and prudent. Then the good fortune of our dynasty will last."

BASIC REQUIREMENTS FOR A GOOD RULER

Taizong told the crown prince that a good ruler must meet certain basic criteria.

"The ruler is the person the people look up to. He should inspire awe and esteem. He should put the interest of the people in the first place. He should be tolerant and magnanimous so as to bind them together. He should be fair and just in decision-making. He should combine authority with benevolence. He should be humble and diligent. He should treat his parents with filial devotion and his ministers with respect. He should practice virtue and righteousness."

WHAT TANG TAIZONG AND HIS ADVISERS TEACH US TODAY

Taizong knew full well that to become a great ruler, he had to overcome his weaknesses and control his desires. To do so, he had to obtain self-knowledge. This he gained through self-examination and through observing other people, who, in his words, served as a mirror in which he saw himself.

He understood his desires might fog his vision, confuse his mind, and cloud his judgment, causing him to make mistakes and suffer from the consequences. But if he could overcome his weaknesses and free himself of his desires, their effects on him would disappear.

As Aristotle said, knowing yourself is the beginning of all wisdom. A leader with self-knowledge is an enlightened person because self-knowledge leads to self-change; self-change leads to external changes; and these changes will enable you to be a successful leader.

Here is a personal anecdote about the power of self-awareness. I used to be impatient, though I didn't recognize that quality in myself. One day I happened to sit next to a palm reader at a dinner party who said he could judge a person's character traits by looking at their hand. I was skeptical, of course, but showed him my hand anyway. The first thing he said was that I was an impatient man. I was struck by his diagnosis. The next moment something inexplicable occurred: I experienced an epiphany—I knew then and there that I would no longer be impatient. The demon had suddenly left me and the spell was broken. To my surprise, I was soon being commended for my patience.

2

On Human Resources

An enlightened ruler employs the wise, giving full play to their wisdom, so that he himself will never be short of wisdom; he employs the talented, giving full play to their talents, so that he himself will never be short of talents.

—HAN FEIZI*

Taizong was a man of destiny, one of great ability and dynamic personality, but he was also uncommonly introspective. He had the good sense to know his limitations. That led him to formulate a wise policy on human resources.

His success was a tribute to the collective wisdom of the emperor and his advisers rather than to his individual genius. It was the result of superior teamwork rather than the performance of a lone virtuoso.

* Han Feizi (c. 280–233 BC) was one of the most influential philosophers of the Warring States period.

TANG TAIZONG AND HIS ADVISERS' WORDS

A SKILLED CARPENTER

Taizong summarized his experience in human resources management for the crown prince as follows.

"An enlightened ruler employs men as a skilled carpenter selects wood. If the wood is straight, he uses it as a shaft for a cart; if it is crooked, he uses it as a wheel. If it is long, he uses it as a roof beam; if it is short, he uses it as a rafter. Straight or crooked, long or short, each piece is useful.

"An enlightened ruler employs men in the same way. He uses the wise man's brain, the stupid man's brawn, the brave man's courage, and the coward's caution. Wise or stupid, brave or cowardly, each person can be employed according to his abilities. Just as a skilled carpenter has no rejected materials, so an enlightened ruler has no wasted human resources. He does not overlook a man's good qualities because of some shortcomings; nor does he forget a man's merits because of minor blemishes.

"Don't use men of great abilities for small jobs; don't use men of small abilities for important tasks. If you place the right people in the right positions, you can run the government smoothly; if you place the wrong people in the wrong positions, you will have endless troubles.

"A wise ruler knows how to judge people and how to make good use of their abilities."

SCOUTING TALENTS

Taizong told the crown prince, "A boat crossing the ocean depends on its sailors. A bird flying through the skies depends on its wings. An emperor running his country depends on the support of his aides. You should rather have one talent in your employ than have a thousand ounces of gold in your coffer.

"But talented people may live in obscurity. They may be waiting for the right opportunity; they may come from humble origins or have low status; they may be poor or holding menial jobs. You must make every effort to seek them out, for such people will make your life easier."

ACQUAINTANCES

Prime Minister Fang Xuanling said to Taizong, "Your old colleagues, including your uncle, are complaining because they haven't received appointments in the new government."

Taizong replied, "As emperor, I must be impartial. I must select those who are qualified for their jobs. Qualification is the only criterion. How can we have one set of criteria for those we know and another for those we don't? I don't forget a man even if I met him only once, to say nothing of those who have worked with me for many years. But if they do not measure up to the standard, they are not up to the job. I can't appoint them just because they are my acquaintances. You only told me about their complaints, but have you examined their abilities?"

SELF-RECOMMENDATION

Taizong said to his ministers, "You don't know many talented people, and I don't know them either. If we just wait and wait, we won't get recruits. What about letting people recommend themselves?"

"No, I don't think that's a good idea," objected Minister Wei Zheng. "Knowing others is not easy; knowing oneself is also difficult. But an ignorant person may regard himself as capable. He may exaggerate his abilities and may be quite good at promoting himself. Therefore, if you let people recommend themselves, you could end up recruiting self-seekers who have no real talent."

TRUE FAIR-MINDEDNESS

Taizong encouraged officials to recommend talented people, but some of them were afraid of being accused of favoritism.

Taizong said to his ministers, "I often hear people say, 'This man is a relative of Minister So-and-So. That man is a friend of General So-and-So.' I want you to know that as long as you are honest in recommending talents, you have nothing to fear. The ancients would not refrain from recommending a worthy man because he was a relative or a friend. Nor would they hesitate to recommend an opponent. That was true fair-mindedness."

When Taizong appointed his brother-in-law Zhangsun Wuji to a senior position, he was criticized for nepotism.

Taizong responded: "To show my concern for my in-law, I could have given him lots of money. But I offered him the job because I wanted to use his talent."

ELEGANT WRITING AND REAL TALENT

Candidates for the civil service had to pass a preliminary and a final examination. There were two well-known scholars in the capital. Taizong had heard of their names but was surprised to find they were not on the roster of successful candidates. He asked Wang Shidan, the chief examiner, about it.

"True, these two men can write elegant essays," Wang replied, "but their language is too flowery and their style too frivolous. Such people don't have real talent. If they are allowed to pass the final, I'm afraid others may emulate them. I don't think that is what Your Majesty expects to see?"

Taizong agreed.

SIX TYPES OF GOOD OFFICIALS

Minister Wei Zheng categorized good officials into six types:

"Those who are prescient enough to tell signs of coming events and take preemptive actions before any trouble occurs so as to protect the ruler.

"Those who give the ruler sound advice, carry out his good policies, and correct his mistakes promptly.

"Those who work hard, inspire the ruler with examples of sage kings in history, and recommend worthy men to him.

"Those who are perceptive, capable of remedying the ruler's mistakes and turning a bad thing into good account.

"Those who abide by the law, do not take bribes or seek high pay, and lead a simple and frugal life.

"Those who do not flatter and dare to speak out against the ruler's mistakes."

SIX TYPES OF BAD OFFICIALS

He also divided wicked officials into six types:

"Those who do not work hard but think only of power and wealth and have no principles.

"Those who always say yes to the ruler, try to please him by any means, and go along with him even when he is wrong.

"Those who are double-faced, jealous of the worthy, and use tricks to manipulate the ruler and cause him to be unfair to his officials.

"Those who are smart enough to conceal their own wrongdoing, are eloquent enough to win favor from others, and purposefully create confusion in court.

"Those who abuse their position for selfish ends and try to feather their own nests in the name of the ruler.

"Those who use artful talk to beguile the ruler, confuse right and wrong to mislead him, and cause him to bear a bad name."

WHAT TANG TAIZONG AND HIS ADVISERS TEACH US TODAY

A key to Taizong's success lay in his shrewd judgment of the strengths and weaknesses of his subordinates and his ability to make the best use of them.

The art of leadership is the art of leveraging—of giving full play to the strengths of others and enabling them to realize their potential.

We can learn the following from Taizong about leadership:

First, leaders don't have to be skilled in every field but they must have an innate ability to assess people.

Second, leaders don't seek perfection in others but are able to identify their talents and gifts.

Third, leaders must have the inner security not to be jealous of other people's talents but, rather, to bring them into full play.

Fourth, leaders must possess self-knowledge so that they can form a team with the right combination of strengths to make up the leader's deficiencies.

Last but not least, leaders must have sufficient integrity to inspire loyalty and respect.

Taizong was greatly admired by the Japanese shogun Ieyasu Tokugawa for his leadership prowess. The latter was the founder of the Tokugawa dynasty in the seventeenth century. Tokugawa made a deep study of *The Zhenguan Executive Guide* under the tutelage of a Sinologist. He used Taizong's ideas to govern and bade his successors to do the same. His dynasty ruled Japan for 264 years.

3

On Moral Character and Talent

A man must have first, a lofty goal; second, a desire for knowledge; and third, a persevering spirit. He will not accept a low standard if he has a lofty goal; he will not be content with a little knowledge if he understands there is no limit to knowledge; and he is bound to succeed whatever his pursuit if he perseveres. Not a single one of these three qualities can he do without.

—ZENG GUOFAN*

Senior Minister and Chief Remonstrant Wei Zheng served at the side of Taizong for seventeen of his twenty-three years as China's emperor. Wei was a talented official, a Confucian scholar, and a man of moral excellence. It wasn't surprising that Taizong sought his opinion on the issue of weighing a man's ability against his integrity.

---

* Zeng Guofan (1811–72) was an eminent scholar, official, and military general who was most responsible for suppressing the Taiping Rebellion in the late Qing dynasty.

TANG TAIZONG AND HIS ADVISERS' WORDS

SETTING EXAMPLES

"I must be careful in appointing officials," Taizong said to his ministers. "The people are watching whom I appoint. If I appoint an honest man, he will set a good example for all. If I appoint a wicked man, he will attract others who are likewise wicked men. I must also be cautious in giving rewards and punishments. If I reward a meritorious official, those with no merits will quit on their own. If I punish a wicked one, others like him will also get the warning."

"It is difficult to appraise a man," Wei Zheng responded. "We have to look into his moral conduct before hiring him. We have to check up on his performance before promoting or demoting him. If we hire a man of mediocre ability, he may not do a good job, but the harm he can do is limited. If we appoint an evil yet capable man, he can cause a lot of damage."

EXAMINATION RESULTS

"We select civil servants based only on the examination results," Taizong said to Vice Prime Minister Du Ruhui, who was in charge of government personnel. "But we know next to nothing about their moral character. If a villain is selected, it may be years before he betrays himself. But by that time even if we punish him, it'll be too late. He will have done damage already. What can we do?"

"In the Han dynasty, candidates had to be recommended by local officials," Du Ruhui replied. "Their knowledge and moral character had already been scrutinized before they were appointed. That's why the Han court was able to recruit a considerable number of men who were both able and virtuous. Now we hold examinations to select civil servants. Thousands of candidates come to the capital each year. Some may pretend to be honest. Some may use fine talk to conceal their inadequacy. It's impossible to know. The system leaves much to be desired."

WHAT TO OBSERVE IN A MAN

Wei Zheng told Taizong, "Before a man achieves recognition, observe whom he is associated with; when he occupies high office, see whom he promotes; when he becomes rich, watch what he accumulates; when he is poor, see what he does not accept; when he is in difficulty, notice what he refuses to do. Make use of his strengths and avoid his weaknesses."

WARTIME VS. PEACETIME

Wei Zheng said, "In wartime, we needed talents desperately and had to recruit whoever was available without paying too much attention to his moral aspect. In peacetime, we should only hire those who are both talented and virtuous."

A GENTLEMAN'S WEAKNESSES

Comparing the weaknesses of a gentleman to the strengths of a villain, Wei Zheng commented, "A villain is not without minor virtues, and a gentleman is not without minor weaknesses. The minor weaknesses of a gentleman are like flaws in a piece of jade. A good merchant won't discard it, because the minor defects don't affect its beauty as a whole. The minor virtues of a villain are like the edge of a blunt knife. It cuts but doesn't cut well. A good craftsman won't be interested because it's basically defective."

SETTING HIGH STANDARDS

Wei Zheng explained: "The reason we have few ministers who are both talented and virtuous is probably that we haven't set high enough standards for them and haven't given them a chance to go through some rigorous tests. If we give them to understand that we have great expectations of them and that patriotism and disinterestedness are ministerial requirements, we'll give them a goal to strive for."

WHAT TANG TAIZONG AND HIS ADVISERS TEACH US TODAY

Moral character was a key criterion for selecting officials in Taizong's court. But Taizong considered it justifiable to recruit capable people in certain circumstances even though their moral conduct fell short of the standard.

The question is, how much consideration should be given to a person's moral conduct and how much to his ability? What should the guidelines be?

To appreciate Taizong's insight on the subject, let's consider three scenarios.

First, the situation is urgent and the task is important, but few people are qualified for the job. In this case, we can rightly argue for hiring somebody who is capable of doing the job yet has questionable ethics. But it should be a rare event.

Second, the pressure is moderately high. A fair number of people are qualified for the job. In this case, we may be justified in hiring somebody who is capable but whose behavior is moderately unethical.

Third, there is no urgency. Many people can do the job. In this instance, we may never be justified in hiring somebody whose conduct is unethical.

In each case, the merits of the goal and the pressure of the situation must be weighed against the demerits of lowering the ethical standard in hiring. As we become conscious of the implications of such trade-offs, we can make better decisions as to what standard we should set under the circumstances rather than have an unrealistic standard or no standard at all.

4

On Management

Before you are a leader, success is all about growing yourself. When you become a leader, success is all about growing others.

—JACK WELCH*

Taizong held daily meetings with his ministers to discuss various issues. Once a policy decision was reached, the Secretariat would draft an imperial order. The draft would be sent to the Chancellery for further deliberation. If there was no objection, it would be forwarded to the Department of State Affairs to execute. The latter controlled the six ministries of finance, defense, justice, civil personnel, public works, and external affairs.

If the Chancellery disagreed with the imperial order, it could either amend or veto it. No imperial order could be carried out without the approval of both the Secretariat and the Chancellery; the Department of State Affairs also

---

* Jack Welch (born in 1935) is the former CEO of GE and one of the most successful business leaders of our time.

had a say. This process reduced possible mistakes as well as provided checks and balances within the government.

TANG TAIZONG AND HIS ADVISERS' WORDS

QUALITY VS. QUANTITY

Taizong told Prime Minister Fang Xuanling, "The key to good governance lies in having an efficient government. The quality of civil servants is more important than the quantity. If we can't find qualified people, let there be vacancies. We can manage with fewer but more talented people. After all, what good is it if we hire a lot of mediocre men? In fact the more mediocre men there are, the more likely things will get messed up."

SAVING FACE

Taizong asked officials in the three departments to think independently, stick to principles, dare to disagree, and not muddle through for the sake of saving face.

He said: "The Secretariat and the Chancellery were set up to check up on each other so as to avoid mistakes. It's quite natural for them to have different opinions. Some opinions are correct, others are not. But those who hold dissenting views share the same objective—to serve the public interest.

"Now, some officials try to gloss over their faults. They

don't like criticism and hate those who speak out. Some officials try to avoid conflicts by all means. Even if they know it is a wrong decision, they choose to obey their superiors because they are afraid if they speak out they will cause their superiors to lose face. This kind of behavior must stop. They must understand it is a minor concern to cause somebody to lose face, but it is a serious matter to jeopardize public interest.

"In the Sui dynasty, many officials took an equivocal attitude on matters of principle. They would say yes to their superior's face but complain behind his back. They thought they were clever and things would never go against them. But they were dead wrong. Disaster struck in the end. These officials suffered badly and were condemned by public opinion."

LOOKING AFTER A PATIENT

Taizong said to his ministers, "Running a country is not very different from looking after a patient. When the patient begins to recover, he needs special care. Any negligence can endanger his life. We've just brought peace and stability to the land, but if we slacken our effort, we can still fail. Living in the palace, it's impossible for me to know everything. I rely on you as my ears and eyes, as my hands and feet. We belong to one body and we should help each other. So speak out if you find something wrong. If we don't trust each other and don't talk honestly, it will be the misfortune of our country."

"I am happy to see our country is at peace," replied Wei Zheng, "but I am even happier to hear what Your Majesty has just said."

SENSE OF PROPORTION

In the beginning, Prime Minster Fang Xuanling and Vice Prime Minister Du Ruhui took everything upon themselves. Taizong was displeased.

"Your role as prime ministers," he told them, "is to share my burden, help me run the government, and be my ears and eyes. But I have heard that you spend a lot of time reviewing hundreds of legal cases. If so, you'll have no time to examine official documents, to say nothing of seeking out worthy men on my behalf."

He thereby ordered that small cases be handled by junior officials; only major cases might be referred to the prime ministers.

THE IMPORTANCE OF DELEGATING

Taizong asked Xiao Yu, former prime minister of the Sui dynasty, about the style of Emperor Wen, founder of the Sui. "What kind of a ruler was he?"

"Emperor Wen was a self-disciplined and hardworking ruler," Xiao Yu replied, "who took his job very seriously. He would hold audience sessions from sunrise till sunset. Sometimes he and his ministers were so engrossed in their discussions that they forgot to eat. He might not have been wise, but he was surely conscientious, trying very hard to be a good ruler."

"You know only part of him," said Taizong. "He thought he was smart, but he was not really wise. He decided on every issue himself, big and small, because he didn't trust his ministers. So even though he exhausted himself, he could not get everything right. Knowing he was a suspicious man, his ministers dared not give him any honest advice. They just agreed with whatever he decided."

Taizong went on to explain his own style. "My style is different. Ours is a big country. We have many issues to deal with every day. They should be thoroughly looked into by officials in relevant departments and then the prime minister will make a recommendation to me. Everybody has his limitations. A ruler must have ministers to assist him. If he has to handle so many issues by himself, he is bound to make mistakes. How can he be right every time? Just think what would happen if five out of ten decisions he makes every day are wrong. Day by day, month by month, his mistakes would accumulate, and sooner or later they would lead to disasters. It is much better to delegate responsibilities to the worthy."

DIRECT IMPACT ON THE PEOPLE

Minister Ma Zhou wrote Taizong a memorandum, which read, "How provincial and county officials do their jobs has a direct impact on the life of the people. We may not obtain the best candidates for each county, but if we select qualified men as provincial governors and prefects, we shall be doing the right thing.

"In ancient times, candidates for ministerial positions had to work as local officials first. Nowadays too much emphasis is placed on central government appointments, but too little attention is given to staffing local posts. The quality of officials in remote regions is even worse. That may be the reason why life is still hard for the people."

Whereupon Taizong announced, "From now on, I shall personally select provincial governors and prefects. And each minister from the fifth rank up will be responsible for recommending a candidate for county magistrate."

He told his ministers, "I often lie awake at night thinking about the affairs of state. What worries me most is whether provincial governors and county magistrates are up to their jobs. Living in the palace, I see and hear only a limited amount. I count on these officials. How well they perform their duties concerns the fate of our country."

A PERVERSE TENDENCY

Minister Wei Zheng wrote a memorandum to Taizong about a perverse tendency he noticed in the emperor.

"Your Majesty is a gifted man, but I've noticed a peculiar tendency in you. When you hear somebody's good points, you tend to discount them. But when you hear somebody's weaknesses, you would readily believe they are true. Why?

"Those who like to find others' faults to attack tend to be mean men; those who like to find others' good points to praise tend to be good men. If you take credit away from people for their shortcomings more than you give credit for their strengths, you will embolden mean men and discourage good men. This is not the way to have a proper relationship with your ministers. On the contrary, it will create a barrier between you and them. And it is bound to impair the smooth running of the government."

LOOKING FOR GOOD POINTS IN THOSE YOU DON'T LIKE

In another memorandum, Wei Zheng wrote, "Your Majesty is willing to forgive some big mistakes of your ministers but is rather intolerant of small errors. A small error can cause you to lose your temper. But you can't run the government according to your personal preferences. Toward those you like, be aware of their shortcomings. Toward those you dislike, look for their strengths. If you can't see good points in those you dislike, good people will be scared. If you can't see weaknesses in those you like, villains will be emboldened."

THE NORM OF GOVERNANCE

Commenting on the way Taizong treated senior and junior officials, Minister Wei Zheng said, "The norm of governance is that senior officials deal with important matters and junior officials deal with less important ones. In appointing officials, Your Majesty rightly pays a lot more attention to senior posts than junior posts. But when something happens, you tend to believe junior officials more than senior officials. Why do you suspect senior officials whom you have carefully chosen yourself?

"Moreover, senior officials should not be punished for making mistakes in handling small matters, and junior officials should not be responsible for making big decisions.

"If avoiding mistakes becomes the objective of civil servants, they will try to cover up their mistakes. That will lead to deceit. Then it will be impossible to have a good government."

Taizong agreed with his minister.

MUTUAL TRUST

Wei Zheng wrote Taizong another memorandum, which read, "Your Majesty appointed worthy men to important posts. You gave them a lot of responsibilities but you did not place enough trust in them. This lack of trust causes them to have misgivings, and misgivings will prevent them from doing a good job. They would just perform their routine tasks perfunctorily, with little sense of duty. And it is impossible to expect them to work toward establishing a long-lasting dynasty.

"If the ruler does not trust his minister, he can't make use of him. If a minister does not trust his ruler, he can't serve him either. Mutual trust is the basis of their working together, and trust is created when neither the ruler nor the minister is guided by self-interest.

"It is no good if a ruler doesn't know how to judge a man. It is no good either if he knows how to judge a man but doesn't know how to use him. It is still no good if he uses him but doesn't trust him."

FATUOUS KING AND CONSCIENTIOUS MINISTERS

Taizong asked, "Which case is worse: the king is fatuous but his ministers are conscientious, or the king is conscientious but his ministers are irresponsible?"

"If the king has good judgment," replied Wei Zheng, "he can tell which minister is good and which one is wicked. Punish the wicked one, and he sends a warning to a hundred others. They won't dare to be careless. If the king is fatuous and headstrong, he won't listen to his ministers. Sooner or later he'll be in trouble."

"King Wen of the Northern Qi dynasty was a tyrant, but his prime minister seemed to have managed well enough. Do you know why?" asked Taizong.

"His prime minister did manage to keep the country from falling apart," answered Wei Zheng. "But it was a very difficult and precarious situation. It is not to be compared with a wise ruler running a country with honest ministers."

DERELICTION OF DUTY

Jia Chong, governor of Daizhou, was accused of dereliction of duty by an imperial censor because one of his subordinates had committed a serious offense.

Taizong rejected the accusation and said, "A father may not be held responsible for the action of his son, nor should a man be held responsible for the action of his brother. If we demote a governor because somebody under him committed a crime, it would encourage officials to cover up crimes. Then real criminals may go unpunished. There are criminals everywhere. It is unreasonable to hold the governor responsible. What you should do is to see that he does a good job investigating the crime and prosecuting the culprit."

LOCUSTS

Taizong knew how to use dramatic gestures to win public recognition, just like a modern politician in front of a television camera.

During the Korean expedition, one of his generals was shot by an arrow. On the battlefield Taizong sucked pus from his wound in front of many soldiers, who were deeply touched by his action.

One year, swarms of locusts descended upon Chang'an. Taizong went to the imperial park to see for himself the damage they had caused.

"Grain is the people's livelihood. But you eat it!" he cursed, picking up a handful of the insects. "Better you eat my heart and lungs!"

As he put his hand to his mouth, his attendants tried to stop him for fear he might get sick. But Taizong insisted on taking a bite.

"I'll eat them for the sake of my people even if I become ill."

And he swallowed them. Legend says the locusts disappeared the next day.

MANAGING STAKEHOLDERS

Taizong gave the crown prince the following advice on the role of stakeholders and their management.

"Our country is too large to be run by one man. As emperor, I need others to help me. That was why I awarded my kinsmen fiefs, so that they have a stake in supporting me to maintain the stability of the empire. But you should not allow stakeholders to become too powerful. Or else you may lose control. If the branch is too large, the tree may break; if the tail is too big, it may wag the dog. Therefore it is better to have a large number of stakeholders but keep their individual power small. This way there will be checks and balances among the stakeholders and you will be able to maintain control. All will be loyal to you."

Efficiency is doing things right. You can enhance efficiency by having fewer but talented people as opposed to having many mediocre people. The more mediocre they are, the less will be accomplished.

Effectiveness is doing the right things. You can enhance effectiveness by encouraging people to voice their opinions so that correct and informed decisions can be made.

You should delegate responsibilities to worthy subordinates. It will not only reduce your workload but enable you to avoid costly mistakes.

You should discourage blind obedience and face-saving behavior at the expense of honesty.

You should be more eager to find others' good points to praise than to find faults to criticize.

You should make people feel they're trusted; they'll do a better job for you.

You should pay attention to those working at the grassroots level because they're perceived as your deputies. Who they are reflects who you are, and how they do their work has a direct impact on the fate of your enterprise or organization.

Taizong's emphasis on the quality of civil servants reminds me of what Lee Kuan Yew, the founding father of Singapore, did to shape that nation's civil service system.

Lee believed that civil servants should be appointed and advanced on the basis of their abilities, effort, and achievements, regardless of race or family background. He also believed that to recruit and retain talents and to maintain a clean, honest government, civil servants should be well paid.

He said, "The task of the leaders must be to provide or create for them a strong framework within which they can learn, work hard, be productive and be rewarded accordingly. And this is not easy to achieve."

Lee linked the pay of top civil servants to that of top professionals in the private sector while at the same time strengthening anticorruption laws to give the government wider power to investigate and prosecute suspected officials and their families.

Perhaps because of their Chinese origin, many Singaporeans like to compare the success of their country to that of Tang China. They consider their meritocratic and highly efficient government a key factor in their country's success.

5

On Remonstrance

Criticism may not be agreeable, but it is necessary. It fulfills the same function as pain in the
human body. It calls attention to an unhealthy
state of things.

—WINSTON CHURCHILL[*]

The duty of the imperial censor in Taizong's government
was to supervise officials; his weapon was impeachment.
He had the authority to investigate complaints and im-
peach any official for violating the law, for miscarriage of
justice, for failing to implement government policies, for
overspending, and so on. But the imperial censor could
be retaliated against if he offended a powerful official.

The duty of the remonstrant was to supervise the monarch; his weapon was public remonstrance. His designated
role was to criticize the monarch for improper behavior

---

[*] Winston Churchill (1874–1965) was a British statesman, orator, author,
and prime minister during World War II, and is regarded as one of the
greatest Britons ever.

and wrong policies. The position was often filled by mentors of the monarch or men of high stature. Although the job was highly prestigious, it carried inherent risk. The remonstrant could become such an irritant that the ruler might turn against him. He could be demoted, dismissed, corporally punished, or even put to death by an intolerant tyrant.

TANG TAIZONG AND HIS ADVISERS' WORDS

SELF-REFLECTION

Taizong said, "I often sit quietly and reflect on myself. I am concerned that what I have done may not be in keeping with the will of Heaven and cause public discontent. I hope to get advice and remonstrance from honest men so that I am not out of touch with the outside world, and so that I can address any complaint in a timely manner."

He told the crown prince about the importance of listening to remonstrance. "The ruler runs the country from the depth of his office. But he cannot see everything he should see and hear every voice he should hear. As a result, if he makes a mistake, he may not know; if he does something wrong, he cannot correct it in time. That is why he needs to hear complaints, heed different views, and listen to other people's advice. If the advice is good, even if it comes from a slave, he should accept it. If the advice is bad, even if it comes from a nobleman, he should reject it. Don't fuss about the details or the style of those who give you good advice."

A FATUOUS RULER

Taizong asked his chief remonstrant, "What is an enlightened ruler and what is a fatuous ruler?"

Wei Zheng replied, "An enlightened ruler listens to different opinions whereas a fatuous ruler listens to only one side. For example, the second emperor of the Qin dynasty listened only to his eunuch minister Zhao Gao. Isolated from other officials, he had no idea that his regime was about to collapse. Emperor Yang of the Sui dynasty listened only to a sycophant minister and didn't know that rebellions were sweeping over the country. If the ruler makes a point of listening to different people, powerful ministers won't be able to hide the truth from him. Information flow won't be blocked. And the voice from below will reach his ears."

His advice won Taizong's hearty consent.

NO WINNER

Taizong said to his ministers, "If a man wants to see himself, he needs a mirror. If a ruler wants to know his own faults, he needs loyal ministers. If he thinks he is smart and his ministers don't point out his mistakes, sooner or later he'll run into trouble.

"When the ruler loses, his ministers will also lose.

Remember how the Sui dynasty was lost? Emperor Yang was a despot. His ministers all kept their mouths shut. Nobody tried to stop his wrongdoings. In the end, he was killed, and his ministers were not spared either. That is a lesson for all of us. If you want to share a peaceful and stable rule with me, you must talk to me frankly and let me know if I've done something wrong. I may not accept your remonstrances right away, but I'll think about them. Then I'll choose which good advice to follow."

IMPERIAL HUNT

Taizong said to his ministers, "Somebody wrote me a memorandum saying I go on hunting expeditions too frequently. At present the empire is at peace, but we should not forget military exercises, which hunting provides. That's why I go hunting in the imperial park with my entourage. We don't cause any trouble to the public. So what's the problem?"

"Since Your Majesty solicits criticisms from officials," replied Wei Zheng, "you have to let them say what they want. If what they suggest has merit, it will benefit the country; if not, no harm is done."

"You have a point there," agreed Taizong.

BEING GENTLE

Taizong asked Wei Zheng, "I have found that when officials write to me, they present their ideas very well. But when they talk to me, they often hem and haw. They can't even speak coherently. Why is that?"

"I know they spend days preparing what to say," explained Wei Zheng. "But in Your Majesty's presence, they become nervous. As a result, they only manage to say one-third of what they wanted to. Please be gentle and empathetic with them, or you'll intimidate them."

"I see," said Taizong. "If they are already nervous when talking about routine business, I can imagine how brave a person must be to come forward and remonstrate with me. If I show any displeasure, I will scare him away and nobody will speak to me frankly. I promise you that in the future I won't get angry even if I don't like what I hear."

PROVOCATIVE LANGUAGE

A magistrate in Henan named Huangfu Dezan wrote Taizong a memorandum criticizing the construction work in Luoyang because it imposed a heavy burden on the people. He described the real estate tax as exploitation of the people and blamed the craze for fancy hairstyles among local women on the ladies in the imperial palace, who set the fashion.

Taizong was incensed. "This is ridiculous! Will he be satisfied if we collect no taxes and if the court ladies all shave their heads?"

He wanted to put the man on trial for slandering.

Wei Zheng objected. "Read one memorandum, and you can feel the author is weeping. Read another, and you can feel the author is sighing. Since ancient times, memoranda have often used provocative words to gain the attention of the reader. Provocative language is somewhat similar to slander, but a sage ruler can find something good even in a madman's remarks. It's up to Your Majesty to decide what's true and what's not in a memorandum."

"Well said," replied Taizong. "Only you can make such a point."

Instead of punishing the magistrate, he awarded him twenty rolls of silk.

SYCOPHANTS

Taizong made the following comment regarding sycophants.

"Flatterers and sycophants are pests. To pursue power and profit, they try to find favor with the ruler through their pleasing talk and ingratiating manner.

"When the ruler is surrounded by such people, his ears and eyes will be blocked. He cannot see his own faults, and loyal officials will not dare to speak out. It is dangerous.

"Wholesome advice often grates on the ear, but it can benefit you. Flattery is often pleasing to the mind, but it can do you harm. The enlightened ruler follows wholesome advice. Even though it may taste bitter, it can cure his sickness. The ignorant ruler likes flattery. Even though it may taste sweet, it can destroy him."

NO TRICKERY OF SUBORDINATES

A townsman asked Taizong to weed out sycophants in the court.

"Those I appointed to office," said Taizong, "are all honest and competent in my judgment. Do you know anyone who is not?"

"No, I don't," answered the man. "But I have an idea how to uncover such people. If Your Majesty pretends to be angry, then we'll know. Those who come forward to remonstrate are upright men, and those who go along with you are sycophants."

Taizong rejected the idea. "Whether a river is clean or not depends on its source," he explained. "I am like the source of a river and my subordinates are like the flow. If I use deceitful means to test them, how can I expect them to be honest? It would be as unreasonable as expecting a river to be clean when its source is muddy. I despise a ruler who uses tricks to test his subordinates. Though your intention is good, your method would damage my credibility."

RESPECTING THE PRIVATE LIFE OF SUBORDINATES

Imperial censors Quan Wanji and Li Renfa liked to ferret out what officials did in their private lives and report it to Taizong. They would lash out at senior officials in public. Taizong appeared to encourage such practices. He granted the two men private audiences and even praised them for "not trying to curry favor with powerful ministers." Many officials became ill at ease.

Wei Zheng was disgusted. "Quan Wanji and Li Renfa are despicable men," he said to Taizong. "They don't know what is important and what is not. They think that exposing others' private lives is something honorable, that informing against your ministers is being loyal to Your Majesty. But among those attacked by them, no one has committed a crime. Your Majesty, of course, knows what kind of men Quan and Li are. That's why you didn't entrust them with important duties. But you still chose to use them because, I guess, you thought their verbal assaults might keep everyone scrupulously honest. As a result, these scoundrels became powerful while loyal ministers are alienated from you. I'm not sure you have promoted many worthy men. However, to be friendly to such villains can only harm your image."

Taizong was at a loss for what to say. Then he awarded Wei Zheng five hundred rolls of silk. Later on, he demoted Quan Wanji and Li Renfa.

THE DILEMMA OF A LOYAL OFFICIAL

"I haven't received much advice from my ministers lately. Do you know why?" Taizong asked Wei Zheng.

"Those you don't trust don't speak out because they fear you may think they slander you. Those you trust don't speak out because they lack a sense of duty. Each has his own motivations. A feeble-minded man, even if he is honest, does not dare to speak out. A man not close to you does not speak out because he doesn't think you would trust him. A man who is only concerned about keeping his position does not speak out because he doesn't want to offend you. As a result, everybody keeps his mouth shut and just drifts along."

"Exactly," Taizong agreed. "I often ponder this problem. I understand their fear. The power of the ruler often poses a dilemma for a loyal minister who wants to speak out yet is afraid of being punished. Well, I'm open-minded. I welcome all honest remonstrances. Tell the ministers I won't punish anyone for speaking out."

A GOOD OFFICIAL VS. A LOYAL OFFICIAL

On another occasion, Wei Zheng said to Taizong: "I hope Your Majesty will let me be a good minister rather than a loyal minister."

"What is the difference between the two?" asked Taizong.

"There is a big difference. A good minister makes a good name for himself for helping his king make wise decisions so that the good fortune of his king may last long. A loyal minister follows his king blindly even if the king is wrong. The king could be killed, the country could be lost, and the minister could die, but he would make a good name for himself for being loyal."

"Well, I hope you'll be a good minister," said Taizong. Wei Zheng then recounted a conversation between

Duke Jing, the ruler of Qi during the Spring and Autumn period, and Yan Ying, his prime minister.

"The duke asked Yan Ying: 'What is a good minister?'

"'A good minister will neither die for his king,' replied Yan Ying, 'nor will he follow him into exile.'

"'Why not?' asked the duke, not understanding. 'If his king treats him well, appointing him to high office and giving him high pay, isn't he supposed to be loyal?'

"'True,' said Yan Ying, 'he should be loyal. If the king had listened to his good advice, disaster would not have come. The king would never have to flee or die. But if the king ignored his advice and then got into trouble, why should he die for him?'"

A HOPELESS SITUATION

Taizong said: "If the king refuses to heed remonstrance, his ministers will not dare to offend him by speaking out. They have to keep their mouths shut. You can't blame them, can you?"

"Well, a loyal minister should not keep silent," responded Vice Prime Minister Du Ruhui, "even if his king doesn't want to listen to him. If the ministers are willing to risk their lives to remonstrate with the king, there is still hope for the country."

"I agree," said Taizong. "If the king goes wrong and his ministers don't remonstrate, it will be a hopeless situation."

REAL ELOQUENCE

In the beginning of his reign, Taizong listened to remonstrances patiently. But gradually his confidence grew into the arrogance of success, and his self-control slipped, especially after the death of Wei Zheng in 643. He would argue with those who criticized him and debate those who disagreed with him. Minister Liu Ji wrote Taizong a memorandum about his behavior.

"Even if Your Majesty is humble enough to ask advice from your subordinates, you may not receive it. But now when they do voice their opinion, you often get into an argument with them, eager to prevail. Who would dare to speak out? Eloquence is not such a virtue as you think. Lao Tzu said real eloquence means talking little, and Chuang Tzu* said truth does not need a lot of argument. Neither of them favors excessive talking. You may win an argument, but you'll lose the goodwill of your ministers. We achieved peace and prosperity not because we were eloquent talkers but because we were down-to-earth doers. Too much talking is also tiring. I hope Your Majesty will devote your energy to work and be as humble as you used to be."

Taizong admitted his mistake. "Yes, I talked too much. I was proud of my debating skill. It made me look down upon others. Thank you for pointing that out."

---

* Chuang Tzu (c. 369–286 BC) was a great Taoist philosopher and a brilliant prose writer.

MIRROR TO THE EMPEROR

Taizong was grief-stricken when Wei Zheng died in the seventeenth year of his reign. He closed the court for an unprecedented five-day mourning period and made the following famous remark.

"Use brass as a mirror, and one can straighten one's clothes; use history as a mirror, and one can discern the causes of the rise and fall of a state; use other people as a mirror, and one can understand one's own strengths and weaknesses. Now, as Wei Zheng is dead, I've lost a precious mirror."

Wei Zheng's reputation is as high today as it was in his own day. Among the traditional scholar-officials, he is celebrated as an exemplary Confucian minister; in folklore, he has become a door god who protects people against evils.

WHAT TANG TAIZONG AND HIS ADVISERS TEACH US TODAY

The office of imperial censor and the practice of issuing remonstrances were distinctive traditions in ancient China aimed at redressing the ills in its institutions.

In a democracy, freedom of expression is valued. The legal system protects people's right to express their frank opinion. However, there are many "fiefs" in a democracy—corporations, hospitals, schools, colleges, government agencies, and charitable organizations—in which "rulers" wield enormous power over the "ruled."

For example, a manager wields pervasive influence over the lives of his subordinates and their families. He is the virtual "lord" in his "fief," with the power to hire, fire, promote, or demote his employees, whose livelihoods depend on him. And dependency makes them vulnerable.

Even if employees know their employer's behavior is illegal or unethical or both, can they really speak their mind? Can they say what they think and not worry about the response of their superiors or peers? Can they be truly honest regardless of self-interest? How likely are they to blow the whistle?

Moreover, how many of today's managers would urge their subordinates to criticize them as Taizong did, to say nothing of rewarding those who speak out?

Reflecting on the government and corporate abuse of power we confront today, I wonder if the remonstrant might not have a deserving place in our society.

6

On Virtues

If there is sincerity in thought, there will be righteousness in the heart; if there is righteousness in the heart, there will be integrity in character; if there is integrity in character, there will be harmony at home; if there is harmony at home, there will be order in the nation; if there is order in the nation, there will be peace in the world.

— *GREAT LEARNING**

Taizong took over the country by force, but he fully agreed with the ancient Chinese belief that a ruler's ultimate legitimacy and authority derive from his virtue and wisdom. When the Mandate of Heaven was granted to a ruler, it meant he was sufficiently wise and virtuous to receive it. Hence he was called the Son of Heaven. But he could lose that right if he failed to fulfill his obligation to rule properly.

---

* *Great Learning* is one of four authoritative books on Confucianism (see footnote on p. 13).

TANG TAIZONG AND HIS ADVISERS' WORDS

POWER VS. VIRTUES

Taizong was discussing the longevity of the Zhou dynasty and the brief life of the Qin dynasty with his ministers.

He said, "King Wu of the Zhou dynasty overthrew the last ruler of the Shang dynasty because the Shang ruler was a tyrant. The first emperor of the Qin dynasty conquered six states and toppled the fading Zhou dynasty. There is little difference in the way the Zhou and Qin were founded, but there is a big difference in their respective life spans."

Minister Xiao Yu responded, "The last ruler of the Shang was a despot. He deserved punishment. That's why King Wu commanded popular support for his uprising. The Zhou dynasty was on the decline, but the six states were innocent. That's why the first emperor of the Qin was not popular in his war of annexation."

"You only understand part of the story," said Taizong. "After taking over the empire, the Zhou ruled by virtue and did many good things for the well-being of the people. So it lasted seven hundred years. But the Qin relied on deceit and brutal force to rule. Its rulers were cruel, dissolute, and extravagant. So its reign was cut short after just two generations. The lesson is this: you may seize power by violence, but you must run the country in a proper way afterward."

Xiao Yu admitted that his understanding was lacking.

"I took over the country by force," Taizong added, "but I must run the country by Confucian virtues."

WEAPONRY

"I checked our armory recently," Prime Minister Fang Xuanling told Taizong. "I found we have more weapons than the Sui dynasty used to have."

"Of course it is important to have sufficient weaponry," responded Taizong. "But I hope you will do a good job to enable the common people to make a decent living. That will be the best weapon to keep us in power. Didn't Emperor Yang have many weapons? But he did not practice benevolence and righteousness. In the end, the people turned their backs on him."

FISH AND WATER

Taizong told his ministers: "If the ruler is righteous but his ministers are not, it is impossible to have a good government. If the ministers are righteous but the ruler is not, it is also impossible to have a good government. When a righteous ruler and honest ministers work closely with one another, it is like fish and water. It will be good fortune for the country."

HEART AS THE SCALES

Taizong said: "A ruler should put the interest of the state above selfish motives and personal considerations. Zhuge

Liang* once said, 'My heart is like the scales. I must be absolutely fair to everybody.' Zhuge Liang felt that way when he was running a small state; how much more must I feel that way running a big country?"

A FAVOR TO YOURSELF

Taizong spoke with his ministers about the importance of being honest in performing their duties.

"I am working hard not only for the common people but also for you. I hope you will enjoy fame and fortune for a long time to come. I hope you will be as fearful of the law of the land as I am of Heaven. Then you will be doing a favor not only for the common people but for yourself as well. An old saying goes: 'Money causes a smart man to lose his willpower and a stupid man to get into trouble.' Corruption is against the law. The culprit may not be uncovered, but he surely lives in fear. The pressure on him will affect his health and even shorten his life. And his children will be ashamed of him, too.

"Birds and fish are caught because they are greedy enough to be tempted by the bait. Those who get into trouble because of their greed are no different from birds and fish, aren't they?"

---

* Zhuge Liang was a famous prime minister of the state of Shu during the Three Kingdoms period.

CONCUBINE

Empress Zhangsun recommended a very pretty girl to Taizong to be his concubine. Much pleased, Taizong was about to inform the girl's family of his intention when Wei Zheng barged in and interrupted, for Wei had found out that the girl was already betrothed to a young man.

"Your Majesty has not bothered to check up on her," he admonished Taizong. "Just imagine how people will gossip!"

Taizong was startled. He immediately ordered the girl to be returned to the young man. But the man denied that they were betrothed.

Taizong was puzzled. "An official may want to curry favor with me, but I don't understand why this man denied his own engagement."

"The man lied because he was afraid," Wei Zheng explained. "Remember what your father did when he set his eyes on a beautiful woman? After he learned she already had a husband working in the palace, he was displeased and transferred the man out of the palace to be a county magistrate. The poor man was frightened out of his wits. By the same token, the girl's betrothed fears that you may find some excuse to punish him in the future."

So Taizong wrote the man a letter, saying it was his fault not to have made inquiries before he accepted the girl.

NINE VIRTUES AND TEN VICES

Wei Zheng wrote a lengthy memorandum to Taizong, listing nine virtues for him to cultivate and ten vices for him to avoid.

"To make a tree grow luxuriantly, we must strengthen its root. To make a river flow a long distance, we must deepen its source. To bring stability to a country, we must lay down a foundation of virtue and benevolence. If the root is not strong, a tree cannot be leafy; if the source is not deep, a river cannot flow far; and if virtue and benevolence are not firmly established, a country won't be stable. I am not very smart but I understand this. An enlightened ruler must understand this point better than I do. Heaven blesses a ruler who does not forget danger in peacetime, who does not indulge in extravagance, who controls his desires, and who practices nine virtues and shuns ten vices."

The nine virtues are as follows:

1 Graciousness
2 Gentleness
3 Respectfulness
4 Prudence
5 Loyalty
6 Fairness
7 Honesty
8 Courage
9 Adherence to principles

The ten vices are the following:

1 Greed. If you like something, know what is enough.
2 Going too far. If you desire something, know where to stop.
3 Arrogance. Remember a high position carries high risk.
4 Overextending yourself. Know the limit of your resources.
5 Indulgence. Exercise self-control.
6 Slackness. Be diligent and consistent.
7 Discouraging your subordinates from speaking out. Listen to them with an open mind.
8 Tolerating slanderers. Oust wicked men from your court.
9 Awarding people when you are happy. The award can be inappropriate.
10 Punishing people when you are angry. The punishment can be too harsh.

WHAT TANG TAIZONG AND HIS ADVISERS TEACH US TODAY

Taizong was greatly influenced by Confucius, who held that political leadership should be centered on virtue. Moral character is a vital guide to a person's fitness to rule. If the Son of Heaven is to rule on behalf of Heaven, then he should model the highest moral standards. He should be the personification of virtues his subjects look up to.

Confucius didn't think moral standards in private life should be any different from those in public life. Rulers can't have one set of standards for private life and another for public life. If they practice virtues in private, they'll most likely exercise them in public. And the responsible execution of public duties requires integrity, which is bound to manifest in their private life.

A ruler's moral values will surely be reflected in his policies and the best ruler is one who holds himself up as a moral example to his followers.

Taizong's emphasis on moral conduct stands in stark contrast to fifteenth- and sixteenth-century Italian political philosopher Niccolò Machiavelli's prescription for keeping "the prince" in power: duplicity, deviousness, manipulation, and brutality. Which approach is right? The Tang dynasty lasted nearly three hundred years. How long were those who followed the counsel of Machiavelli able to keep themselves in power? The answer is self-evident.

7

On the Art of War

The best commander carries out his assignment
with meticulous planning and flawless teamwork;
he is self-possessed — neither is he easily excited by
his superiors, nor is he easily upset by his enemy;
and he acts consistently from the beginning to
the end.

—XUNZI*

Defense Minister Li Jing was Tang Taizong's best general.
A military genius with an illustrious career, Li Jing was
later deified as a celestial warrior in *Romance of the Gods*,
a well-known Ming mythological fiction. A hero of many
victories and a brilliant strategist himself, Taizong enjoyed
discussing the art of war with the general.

* Xunzi (c. 313–238 BC) was a preeminent Confucian philosopher of
the Warring States period.

MINGLE TACTICS

Taizong said to Defense Minister Li Jing, "I've read many books on military strategy, and not one has surpassed Sun Tzu's *The Art of War*. The essence of his teaching is that you will win if you know your strengths and weaknesses and those of your enemy. Many of our generals talk about attacking the weak spots of the enemy and avoiding its strong points. But when it comes to real battles, few can tell what strengths and weaknesses the enemy has because they are being manipulated by the enemy. Please teach our generals how to assess the enemy correctly."

Li Jing replied: "I'll first teach them how to mingle the tactics of a regular attack with that of a surprise attack. Then I'll tell them how strengths and weaknesses can both be feinted. Because if they don't understand how to mix surprise attacks with regular ones, they won't be able to see through the facade of the enemy."

MANIPULATE THE ENEMY

Taizong said: "A good general may engage the enemy forces in a skirmish, which he doesn't need to win. The purpose is to sound out the enemy so that the general can decide what tactics to adopt in the battlefield. We can't do much about the enemy's strengths or weaknesses, but we can change our tactics."

Li Jing replied: "A normal battle repels the enemy. It is a surprise attack that wins victory for you. If the enemy is strong, use a strong force to attack it directly. If the enemy has a vulnerable spot, use a surprise attack to break it. However, if a general doesn't know how to combine regular tactics with surprise maneuvers, he won't be able to defeat the enemy even if he knows its strengths and weaknesses. That's why I want first to teach the generals how to vary their tactics."

Taizong said: "Make sure they understand: If the enemy expects us to launch an open attack, we'll make a surprise foray. If it expects us to mount a flank assault, we'll engage it in a frontal battle. Take the initiative in our own hands and keep the opponent guessing."

Li Jing replied: "Yes indeed, Your Majesty. Manipulate the enemy, but don't be manipulated. I'll elaborate this principle in my lecture."

INDUCE THE ENEMY TO MAKE MISTAKES

Taizong said to Li Jing, "I've read many books on the art of war, and it all boils down to one point: do whatever you can to cause the enemy to make mistakes."

Li Jing replied: "Exactly. If the enemy does not make a mistake, how can we win? When both sides are equal in strength, it will be like playing chess. If one side makes a wrong move, he is bound to lose the game. Look at the outcome of many ancient and modern wars, and you can see that a single misstep often leads to an irretrievable defeat, to say nothing of making *many* mistakes."

SEIZE THE OPPORTUNITY

Taizong asked Li Jing, "Attacking and defending are two different things, but do they follow the same principle? Sun Tzu said: 'If you are good at the former, your enemy won't know how to defend; if you are good at the latter, your enemy won't know how to attack.' What about the enemy attacking us and we also attacking it? What about our taking up a defensive position and the enemy doing the same? What shall we do then? Sun Tzu never said anything about this possibility."

Li Jing replied: "There are many examples in history in which both sides opted to attack or both opted to defend. It is generally accepted that you should attack if you have sufficient power and defend if you don't. Sufficient power is interpreted as strength and insufficient power as weakness. That is an incorrect interpretation of what Sun Tzu really meant.

"Sun Tzu said: 'When you cannot win, take up a defensive position; when you can win, attack.' What he meant was that the decision to attack or defend depends more on whether you have the opportunity to win than on whether you have superior forces. Many readers misunderstand this point, so they attack when they should defend, and defend when they should attack."

DECEIVE THE ENEMY

Taizong continued, "Warfare is essentially based on deception, that is, hide your real intention and keep the enemy guessing. If you want the enemy to attack, pretend you are inferior, and then beat the enemy when it attacks. If you want to put the enemy on the defensive, pretend you have superior forces even if you don't. Do your best to confuse the enemy so that it does not know how to attack and how to defend."

Li Jing agreed. "Exactly, Your Majesty. Attack can serve as an effective defense, and a defensive position can also be used to attack. The two strategies should not be considered in isolation, because both serve one and the same end—victory. If a person cannot grasp this point, what good is it even though he can recite Sun Tzu's book?"

KNOW YOURSELF

Taizong said, "A country may be big, but if it loves war, it is bound to perish. A country may live in peace, but if it fails to prepare for war, it will put itself at risk. We need to have both offensive and defensive strategies, don't we?"

Li Jing agreed. "Yes indeed, Your Majesty. An offensive strategy doesn't just mean attacking the enemy's military position; it also means waging a psychological war to undermine its morale. A defensive strategy doesn't just mean fortifying our walls and fortresses; it also means keeping up the spirits of our troops and heightening our vigilance.

A king should understand this. A general should also understand this. To wage an effective psychological war, you need to know your enemy well, and to keep up your own spirit, you must understand yourself well."

KNOW YOUR ENEMY

Taizong said: "Before a battle, I always try to anticipate the action of the enemy and formulate my strategy accordingly. To do that, I have to understand the enemy's way of thinking. I also try to judge its morale and compare it with ours. And to do that, I have to know my own troops well. The essence of the art of war is to know both yourself and your enemy. Even if you don't know the enemy, as long as you know yourself well, you already have an advantage."

Li Jing replied: "Placing yourself first in an impregnable position, as Sun Tzu said, means knowing yourself well. Waiting for the opportune moment to defeat the enemy means knowing your enemy well. Your defense is largely a function of your own effort, whereas to defeat the enemy, you have to wait for the opportunity provided by its own mistakes. This is up to the enemy. This point cannot be overemphasized."

HOW TO AVOID FIGHTING

Taizong asked: "How can you avoid fighting when two armies are already facing each other?"

Li Jing answered, "If both sides are restrained and well disciplined, fighting won't easily break out. Both sides may withdraw in an orderly manner. Sun Tzu told us not to attack a well-prepared enemy. When both sides are equal in strength, whoever makes a mistake is liable to be taken advantage of, and that may lead to defeat. There are times when we must fight and times when we must not. It's up to us not to fight, but it's up to the enemy to give us the chance to fight and win."

Taizong asked: "What do you mean that it's up to us not to fight?"

Li replied: "If we don't want to fight, we'll position ourselves in such a way that the enemy doesn't know how to engage us in a battle. Even if the enemy commander is capable, he won't be able to carry out his plan. That's why it is up to us not to create any opportunity for the enemy to fight us.

"Sun Tzu said: 'Give the enemy some minor advantage and lure it out, then ambush it. Provoke the enemy and then attack. Encourage it to be complacent by pretending you are inferior and then defeat it. Put up a false front to induce the enemy to act the way you want.' If the enemy commander is not capable, he may well be played into your hands and give you an opportunity to defeat his forces. That's why it is up to the enemy to let us fight and win."

Taizong commented: "I see. This advice is very instructive. So it all depends on whether you adopt the right strategy."

BE EFFECTIVE IN COMBAT

Taizong asked Li Jing, "What did Sun Tzu say about maintaining and enhancing the fighting capacity of our troops?"

Li replied: "'Stay near the battlefield and wait for the enemy to come from afar; give your troops sufficient rest and wait for the enemy, who is fatigued; and feed your troops well, and wait for the enemy, who is hungry.' These are general principles laid down by Sun Tzu upon which we can expand. Use enticement to lure the enemy; keep calm in the face of an impetuous enemy; be steady in the face of a reckless enemy; enforce strict discipline when the enemy becomes lax; maintain good order when the enemy is in chaos; and entrench your position when the enemy attacks. These are ways to maintain and enhance our combat effectiveness."

Taizong commented: "Many people can recite Sun Tzu. But few understand him well enough to extend his basic principles creatively. Please teach our generals how to keep up effectiveness in combat."

STRIVE TO BE HOST RATHER THAN GUEST

Taizong asked his minister, "Why is it better to be a 'host' than a 'guest' in a war? Why is a speedy war better than a protracted one?"

Li Jing replied: "War is the last resort when all other means have been exhausted. If we invade another country and fight like a 'guest' in a distant land, it's impossible to sustain the war for long. Logistical support and the transportation of provisions will be costly, and the burden on the people will be grave. It's definitely a disadvantage not fighting on our own terrain and on our own terms. Sun Tzu said: 'A good commander does not put himself in a position where he has to conscript twice and transport supplies a third time.' This means we should not fight a protracted war. But I've studied his guest vs. host theory and come up with an idea to overcome such a disadvantage."

"What is it?"

"It is to turn the 'guest' into a 'host.' In other words, we'll use the local resources of the enemy to provide for our troops and deprive the enemy of supplies in its own land. Then we'll turn our disadvantage into advantage. What matters is not whether we are a 'guest' or a 'host,' or whether we are fighting a speedy or a protracted war. It is how we approach the situation. And taking the initiative into our own hands is the most important thing."

FORM AN EMOTIONAL BOND

Taizong said to his defense minister: "I was told to use harsh law and severe punishment to make soldiers fear me more than they fear the enemy when they fight. But I'm not so sure. Emperor Guangwu of the Han dynasty was up against an overwhelming enemy force. He didn't use harsh discipline on his army, but in the end, his army won out. How do you explain this?"

Li Jing replied: "The outcome of a war depends on

many factors. It can't be attributed to one thing. Emperor Guangwu had popular support. His opponent didn't understand the art of war, relying too much on the sheer number of his troops, and thereby courted defeat.

"Sun Tzu said: 'You may alienate your soldiers if you punish them before they have a chance to get to know you and develop loyalty to you. But if you fail to enforce discipline on those who have violated rules and regulations, you will not have good soldiers.' In other words, a good general must first establish an emotional bond with his soldiers, and then punish them if necessary. If you only use punishment without first showing that you care for them, you won't succeed."

Taizong said: "But the *Book of Documents** says: 'If the law precedes the emotional bond, it will lead to success. If the emotional bond precedes the law, it will result in failure.' How do you interpret that contradiction?"

Li Jing replied: "Always form an emotional bond first and not the other way around. If you let the law take the first place, it will be difficult to win the hearts of your soldiers. Sun Tzu's words are the absolute truth."

CONTROL YOURSELF

Taizong asked Li Jing: "We have three outstanding generals — Li Ji, Li Daozong, and Xue Wanche. Li Daozong is my

---

* The *Book of Documents* is one of the five classics that form part of the Confucian canon (see footnote on p. 13).

relative. Which one of the other two can be promoted to a more responsible position?"

Li Jing replied: "Your Majesty once told me that Li Ji hadn't won a great victory or suffered a great defeat in his career, while Xue Wanche was capable of either winning big or losing big. In my opinion, that an army neither seeks major victory nor suffers big defeat means that it is highly disciplined. An army capable of winning great victories or suffering big defeats seems to rely too much on chance. That's why Sun Tzu said: 'A good general must first put himself in an impregnable position, then wait for the right moment to defeat the enemy.' And he must exercise discipline and self-restraint."

WHAT TANG TAIZONG AND HIS ADVISERS TEACH US TODAY

Obviously, the principles of the art of war that Taizong and General Li Jing talked about can be applied to modern-day war and business competition, as well as, for that matter, any type of conflict or competitive activity, be it a sports contest, legal battle, or political campaign.

Of the many points the two men so cogently made, I find their discussion of the difference between Generals Li Ji and Xue Wanche most instructive. It shows that risk management is not a uniquely modern concept.

Our attitude toward risk has changed little since ancient times: we're more sensitive to negative outcomes than positive ones; we're not so much risk-averse as we are loss-averse; the more that is at stake, the more risk-averse we tend to be.

Suppose Li Ji and Xue Wanche are investment managers. Whom would you choose to manage your assets? Would it be Li Ji, whose past record shows a stable but not stellar performance, or Xue Wanche, whose style may bring you either high returns or heavy losses?

You may let Li Ji manage a large portion of your assets and Xue Wanche a small portion because you feel you'll have a cushion to absorb some losses while at the same time stand a chance to win big. But suppose you have to choose one man to manage all your assets. Whom would you choose?

We can readily apply the art of war to investment, in which the cardinal principle is: first, don't lose money; and then, try to make gains with good timing. To win victory—that is, to earn a long-term superior return—we must exercise discipline and self-restraint.

8

On Crime and Punishment

If you govern the people by law and force them to
behave by punishment, they will try to keep out
of jail but will have no sense of shame.

If you lead the people by virtue and guide them
with the rules of proper conduct, they will know
shame and become good citizens.

— CONFUCIUS

As soon as he ascended the throne, Taizong set about
reforming the laws, which he considered too strict. He
shared Wei Zheng's view that strict laws were necessary
during times of trouble, but laws should be compassionate
and lenient during times of peace.

To Taizong, law was not an end but a means to an end,
i.e., to foster moral values, for good morals are preventive —
they turn a man away from evil before he has the chance
to commit it — whereas law is punitive. It only comes into
action to punish a man for evil *already* committed.

TANG TAIZONG AND HIS ADVISERS' WORDS

THE ROOT CAUSE OF CRIME

When Taizong discussed with his ministers ways to reduce crime, an official suggested that law enforcement be strengthened and punishment made harsher.

Taizong disagreed. "I believe most people are driven to crime by heavy taxes and corvée* duties or by the extortion of corrupt officials. When they can't keep body and soul together, people will lose their sense of shame. We should cut government expenditures, reduce taxes and corvée duties, and appoint honest officials. If people can earn a decent livelihood and have some savings, crime will naturally decrease. Why do we need harsh laws?"

HARSH JUDGES

Each month the supreme court sent the emperor a report on the number of prisoners in the country and their offenses. Taizong noticed a tendency among the judges to inflict severe punishment on criminals.

"Some cases may have mitigating circumstances," Taizong said to his ministers. "The judges could have been more lenient. A dead man cannot be revived. Coffin makers

---

* Corvée was unpaid, compulsory labor on public projects that was required by the state.

wish a plague to occur every year, not because they hate people, but because they want to sell more coffins. Judges like to give harsh sentences because they want to get good performance appraisals for themselves. How can we correct such a tendency?"

"Appoint upright men to be judges," Minister Wang Gui suggested, "and base their pay increases and promotions on being fair, not on being eager to inflict stiff punishment."

Taizong adopted his proposal and instructed that cases of capital punishment must be reviewed by three officials to avoid a miscarriage of justice.

NO AMNESTY

Although Taizong believed in lenient laws, he didn't favor amnesty. He said: "Amnesty means good luck to criminals but misfortune to victims and innocent people. If there are two amnesties a year, all law-abiding people will be scared. Allow weeds to survive and you'll harm crops. Give criminals a pardon and you'll injure innocent people. That's why I rarely grant amnesty, for fear criminals may think they can get away with breaking the law."

The only time Taizong granted amnesty was when he took pity on 390 death-row convicts and sent them home on condition that they come back in the fall of the next year to be executed. All of the convicts returned to their prisons on time. Taizong was so pleased that for once he pardoned all of them.

SHAMING

General Zhangsun Shunde was found to have accepted bribes in the form of rolls of fine silk. Considering that he'd rendered meritorious services in the past, Taizong decided to punish him differently. He awarded the general a few rolls of fine silk before the entire court.

"The man ought to be punished," protested Hu Yan, vice president of the supreme court. "Why did Your Majesty reward him?"

"If the man has a sense of shame," replied Taizong, "he will understand my message. To make him accept silk this way is a public humiliation. The effect on him is more severe than normal punishment. If he has no sense of shame, then he is just an animal. What's the point of killing an animal?"

AVOIDING SUSPICION

Taizong's wife had lost her parents when she was small. She and her brother had been brought up by their stepbrother, who was an alcoholic. He mistreated them and eventually drove them out of their home.

But she forgave him. She even asked Taizong to give him a job. The man, however, was an ingrate. Not only did he refuse to mend his ways, but he joined a group plotting against Taizong. So he was arrested and sentenced to death.

On the day of his execution, the empress intervened and said to her husband, "His crime is certainly punishable by death. But if he is executed, many people who know he mistreated me in the past may interpret it as my personal revenge. That will hurt your reputation."

Thereupon Taizong spared the man's life.

NOT ENSNARING SUBORDINATES

As bribery in the government increased, Taizong became concerned. He wanted to punish a few corrupt officials severely to send a warning to everyone. He secretly instructed his aides to bribe some officials so as to catch them. A customs officer was arrested after accepting a roll of fine silk. Taizong wanted him to be put to death.

Minister Pei Ju objected. "Taking bribes is a crime punishable by death. There is no question about it. But the difference in this case is that it was Your Majesty who instructed your aide to ensnare him with a bribe. Trapping people this way is hardly appropriate for a ruler. It's obviously against the teaching of Confucius, who told us 'to lead others by virtues and guide them with the rules of proper conduct.'"

Taizong accepted the minister's argument and spared the man's life.

MERITS VS. DEMERITS

In 639, the Chinese army, led by Generals Hou Junji and Xue Wanjun, conquered the kingdom of Gaochang (Karakhoja). The whole country cheered their victory.

However, it became known that General Hou had taken illegal possession of treasures in Gaochang and that his soldiers, following suit, had extensively looted the capital city of Gaochang. General Hou was impeached, arrested, and thrown into prison.

Cen Wenben, vice president of the legislature, wrote Taizong a memorandum expressing his concern. "We celebrated the victory of General Hou just ten days ago. If you court-martial him now, people will think Your Majesty only remembers a man's faults, not his merits.

"When you send a general on a military expedition, the single most important requirement for him is to win victory. If he does so, he should be rewarded even if he commits a corrupt act. If he is defeated, he should be punished even if he is honest.

"Most generals love money. Few are perfectly honest. Make use of their bravery and their brains as well as their greed and stupidity. The smart ones want to make a name for themselves. The brave want to demonstrate their courage. The greedy and stupid go after treasures at the risk of their own lives.

"I hope you will forgive General Hou on account of his accomplishments and continue to use him in the future. You may have to bend the law a little bit, but you'll manifest your magnanimity. Pardoning the general will make him realize his fault all the more deeply."

Taizong accepted his minister's advice and ordered the general to be released.

PERSONAL FEELINGS

Taizong said to the crown prince, "Don't punish a person if he goes against your will, yet what he does is good for the country. Don't reward a person if he pleases you personally, yet what he does is not in the best interest of the country."

DECENCY

General Xue Wanjun was accused of raping a woman of Gaochang. He denied the charge. Taizong wanted to bring the woman to the court to confront the general.

Wei Zheng opposed him. "The general and his brother are highly respected military commanders of our country. It is utterly inappropriate to allow a woman of a conquered country to confront a senior Chinese general in public over so distasteful a matter as fornication. If the accusation is true, your gain will be small. But if it turns out to be false, your loss will be great."

He quoted some historical examples of how the clemency and magnanimity of the ruler were rewarded by the loyalty and devotion of his subordinates and persuaded Taizong to set the general free.

The following is one instructive story from the Spring and Autumn period that was used by Wei in his argument.

A Ribbon-Ripping Banquet

King Zhuang of Chu was giving a banquet for his ministers and generals. Music was playing and toasts were exchanged amid a convivial atmosphere. The banquet went from afternoon into evening and candles were lit. The king asked his concubine, the beautiful Princess Xu, to walk around the hall and pour wine for each guest at the table.

In the midst of laughter and tinkling of cups, a wind suddenly blew out all the candles, and the banquet hall was enveloped in darkness. Princess Xu happened to stand near a man who, enticed by her beauty, pulled at her clothes until his fingers nearly touched her breast. The princess staved off the intrusion dexterously and ripped the chin ribbon off the man's hat.

She ran up to the king and whispered, "Somebody was trying to pull off my clothes. But I've snatched the chin ribbon off his hat. Please have the candles relit. I can identify him easily."

Instead of summoning the attendants to light up the candles, the king proposed that everyone take off his hat, loosen his clothes, and have a good time. Too willing to oblige, the guests complied right away. When the candles were relit, Princess Xu was unable to identify the man. She was upset.

When the party was over, the king explained to her, "That man must've been a little drunk. You needn't make a fuss to spoil the party. These men have worked for me in good faith. I wanted them to have a good time."

Three years went by. War broke out between Chu and its neighbor, Wu. King Zhuang was surrounded by the enemy in a battle and fought desperately to break out. At this moment, one General Tang rushed to his rescue. The general fought so bravely that the king was able to snatch victory out of defeat.

King Zhuang was filled with gratitude. "I haven't been particularly favorable to you, why did you fight so hard to save me?"

He wanted to reward the general, but the general declined his offer.

"Your Majesty, I am the man who harassed Princess Xu at a banquet three years ago. You could have punished me, but you overlooked my fault. From that day on I've been looking for a chance to express my gratitude."

The king's handling of the situation was hailed as a quintessential example of being magnanimous to one's subordinates. Such magnanimity earned him their lasting loyalty.

WHAT TANG TAIZONG AND HIS ADVISERS TEACH US TODAY

Taizong didn't rigidly adhere to the letter of the law. He turned his power to punish and pardon into a management tool.

He conveyed both leniency and condemnation by publicly giving an official the very goods that he'd accepted as a bribe.

He let common sense override law by forgiving an offending general who'd rendered meritorious services.

He pardoned an old colleague and apologized for doing so to demonstrate both his humanity and his respect for the law.

He curtailed corruption by letting officials watch the execution of their corrupt colleagues.

By judiciously exercising his authority, Taizong tried to create an environment that was conducive to good conduct and favorable to cultivating good morals.

If a society honors solely the letter of the law, it risks being too rigid; it risks discounting humanity and common sense. It is the spirit and not the form of law that keeps justice alive.

Today, every organization has its own rules and regulations. It is up to the leader of the organization to make them into an effective management tool and thereby promote desirable organizational behavior.

It should be noted that, while Wei Zheng's advice concerning women may smack of male superiority, in fact, women enjoyed higher status in Tang China than ever before. They were free to love, free to marry, free to divorce and remarry. They had the right to inherit property, which was unprecedented in a traditionally patriarchal society. They could play sports like their male counterparts. While they could not attend school like men, they received education at home. It was such an open-minded attitude toward women that led a concubine of Taizong's to become his daughter-in-law, and eventually, the only female emperor in Chinese history, who was known as Empress Wu.

9

On Frugality

The best government is the one that does not make
its presence felt. The second best is the one that is
praised by the people. The next is the one feared
by the people. The worst is the one despised and
distrusted by the people.

—LAO TZU

The bureaucracy had become bloated under Taizong's
father, who'd rewarded many supporters and relatives by
creating unnecessary positions. Taizong made an effort to
trim the civil service, reducing the number of officials in
the central government from more than two thousand to six
hundred and forty. He downsized provincial bureaucracy by
combining prefectures and counties on a large scale. Taizong also reduced taxes, corvée duties, and military service
by cutting the spending of the imperial family, curtailing
construction works, and refraining from military adventure.

These steps stemmed from his belief that if the people
had a stable life with adequate income, his regime would
be stable, and vice versa.

TANG TAIZONG AND HIS ADVISERS' WORDS

KEEP SUFFICIENT RESERVES

Taizong told the crown prince about the importance of saving. He said, "If a country does not have nine years' grain reserves, there won't be a sufficient amount to guard against natural disasters. If a family does not have one year's supply of clothing, there won't be a sufficient amount to protect against weather changes.

"That is why we should avoid wasteful spending and shun extravagance, and why we must promote agriculture and encourage the people to work hard.

"Sage kings of the past lived frugally despite their exalted status and the wealth at their disposal, not because they disliked the comforts of luxury but because they wanted to promote thrift by example."

LET WEALTH STAY WITH THE PEOPLE

Taizong said to Minister Wang Gui, "We should save up enough grain for possible lean years but no more. The right way to run a country is to let wealth stay with the people, not with the state. Emperor Yang of the Sui had much wealth in his treasury and much grain in his warehouse. But he still lost power. Just as the ancients said, 'If the people don't have enough to live on, how can the ruler survive for long?' Too much wealth accumulated by the state will only tempt the ruler to spend it on himself. And this, in turn, will lead to his ruin."

FOOD IS THE FIRST PRIORITY

"Food is the first concern of the people," Taizong said. "Agriculture is the first priority of our economy. Timing is vital to farming. The ruler must not do anything to cause the people to miss the sowing and harvesting seasons, such as waging wars or building palaces."

Minister Wang Gui concurred: "That's the lesson we learned from the fall of the Sui dynasty. Your Majesty witnessed the event firsthand and knows what changes we should make. But it is easy to have a good start and hard to stick to it."

"It falls on me to carry it through," replied Taizong. "I will restrain myself from doing things that will disturb the people's life."

WAR IS THE LAST RESORT

Taizong said, "Weapons are ominous instruments. A country may have vast territory, but if the ruler is warlike, he will sap its resources. A country may be at peace, but if the ruler is not prepared against war, he can put it in danger.

"You cannot abandon war as a means of defense, but you should not resort to it too often."

PRUDENCE PREVAILS

Kangju, a remote kingdom located in present-day Uzbeki-stan in Central Asia, asked to become a vassal of the Tang empire. Taizong turned down its request.

He said to his ministers, "If Kangju becomes our vassal, it will obligate us to come to its aid if it is invaded. I'll have to dispatch an expeditionary army. It will be a big burden on our people. But what gains will we get for our pains? Only vainglory. No, this is not what I want."

LIVE FRUGALLY

Taizong said, "The ruler should practice frugality so that the people are not overburdened. He should keep gov-ernment activities to a minimum so that the people are not disturbed.

"If the ruler is after pleasure and luxury, he will waste resources. He is bound to alienate himself from the people and incur resentment. His regime may collapse before he can really enjoy being a ruler."

WHAT TANG TAIZONG AND HIS ADVISERS TEACH US TODAY

Taizong preferred simpler government to big government. A student of history and human nature, he knew that there are people who love to wield power over others and that bureaucracy has a tendency to amass power. But big government is expensive, wasteful, and inefficient. Big government means high taxes. High taxes mean less money for people to spend; they slow the economy and incur popular discontent.

Taizong sounded like Benjamin Franklin when he talked about the virtues of saving, frugality, and prudence. He would have been horrified had Tang China run into debt and kept on borrowing, as many countries do these days.

If you live in a country with mounting government debt and are concerned about the future, you may want to consider promoting the virtues Taizong stressed.

10

On the Rise and Fall of an Empire

Danger occurs when you believe you are safe;
decline begins when you think your prosperity
will last long; and disorder sets in when you think
you are in control. Therefore, a gentleman often
reminds himself not to be complacent so as to
keep his good fortune.

—*BOOK OF CHANGES**

Taizong had a penchant for history. He regarded history
as a mirror in which he could see the fate of his own
dynasty. He liked studying the careers of his counterparts
in history, and his concern over his historical image had
a great impact on his policies and his behavior.

---

* The *Book of Changes* is one of the five classics that form part of the
Confucian canon (see footnote on p. 13).

TANG TAIZONG AND HIS ADVISERS' WORDS

KEEPING VICTORY

"Which is more difficult: founding a dynasty or preserving it?" Taizong asked his ministers.

"When an old dynasty is breaking down," replied Prime Minister Fang Xuanling, "many outstanding men rise to contend for the throne. The strong man beats the weak one. The defeated surrenders to the victor. And the victor has to eliminate his opponents one by one. In that sense, founding a new dynasty is very difficult."

"No, I don't think so," disagreed Minister Wei Zheng. "Overthrowing an old dynasty is not that difficult because it's already decaying and losing popular support. The victor has the Mandate of Heaven. But after founding a new dynasty, the victor tends to become complacent. He is likely to indulge himself, likely to increase taxes and corvée duties on the people, and in doing so, likely to make their life miserable again. There he will sow the seeds of decline. From this perspective, preserving victory is more difficult."

"Fang Xuanling went through a lot of hardships with me," said Taizong, "when we were fighting for power. He knew how lucky we were to gain the final victory. Wei Zheng joined me afterward. He concentrated on consolidating the new regime, worrying about what would have happened if we had repeated the mistakes of those we overthrew. He experienced many difficulties in the process.

Now that the task of founding the dynasty is behind us, let us keep up the momentum and work together to make our victory a lasting one."

CAUTION IN TIMES OF PEACE AND PROSPERITY

"It seemed the fortune of past rulers moved in cycles," Taizong remarked to his ministers. "A period of prosperity was invariably followed by a period of decline just as day is followed by night. When the ruler was surrounded by sycophants, his ears and eyes were blocked. He could not see his own faults, and his officials dared not speak out. Sooner or later, he would fall."

"Since ancient times," responded Wei Zheng, "rulers lost power because they had overlooked danger when living in peace, and forgotten the possibility of chaos when everything seemed in good order. Your Majesty is ruling a country that enjoys peace and prosperity, but you must still be cautious, as cautious as though you were treading on thin ice, so to speak. Then the good fortune of our country will last long."

SELF-RESTRAINT

"Some dynasties lasted ten generations," Taizong said to Wei Zheng. "Some lasted only one or two generations. There are also cases in which the same man managed to seize power and then lose it. I am worried that I may become complacent and lose self-restraint before I know it. Do you have any suggestions to prevent that?"

"Every ruler wants to pass his scepter on to his children, grandchildren, and so on," replied Wei Zheng. "History shows that at the beginning of his reign a ruler will recruit virtuous men, live frugally, and encourage remonstrance. But after a while he will depart from those principles. Virtue will give way to emotion. Propriety will be compromised by desires.

"It's not hard to understand what is right, but it's hard to practice what is right, and even harder to carry it through to the end. Everybody has desires. The difference is that the wise man controls himself and doesn't allow himself to go beyond certain limits, whereas the fatuous man is swayed by emotion and doesn't know how to control himself. If Your Majesty exercises self-restraint through to the end, I'm sure your dynasty will last for many generations."

MUTUAL RESPONSIBILITY

"I wonder if the downfall of Sui was Emperor Yang's fault alone," Taizong said to Zhangsun Wuji, his brother-in-law. "His ministers were very irresponsible. They were highly paid and highly placed, but all they did was flatter and mislead. That's why the regime was short-lived."

"Sui collapsed because the emperor wouldn't allow any honest talk in the court," replied Zhangsun. "His ministers were concerned only about keeping their own positions. So they did not remonstrate with him, and they concealed the bad news from him even when uprisings were raging all over the country. Sui's fall is not just a matter of Heaven's will. It was the inevitable consequence of the ruler and his ministers failing each other."

Wei Zheng commented on the same topic in a memorandum: "History shows that a new ruler always works hard and aims high. But after he has made some achievements, he becomes complacent and does not keep up his enterprising spirit. The same is true of his ministers. In the beginning, they are devoted to helping the ruler. But after they have obtained fame and fortune, they become more concerned about keeping their positions than about being worthy of their positions. Their loyalty slips."

AWARENESS OF DANGER

Taizong asked: "Is it difficult for the ruler to keep his power?"

"Very difficult," replied Wei Zheng.

"But all we need to do is to recruit worthy men and listen to their advice. How can that be difficult?"

"History tells us," explained Wei Zheng, "when a ruler is faced with danger, he is likely to appoint worthy men and follow their advice. But when life is happy and peaceful, he tends to slacken off and discourage honest talk in his court. Day by day, month by month, his regime will go downhill until finally its survival is at stake. To prevent that from happening, a wise ruler must be mindful of possible danger even in times of peace. But it is very difficult to think of bad times when you are living in good times, isn't it?"

PRECAUTIONS AGAINST SLIPPING

"Would you like to comment on my performance?" Taizong asked Wei Zheng.

"Your Majesty has been on the throne for more than ten years. Our country is rich and powerful, our territory has increased, and many foreign countries come to pay us their respects. Your Majesty is more prestigious than ever. But you are lagging behind your earlier years in terms of virtues."

"How can that be?" asked Taizong.

"You used to cherish virtues. Now you've become arrogant and self-satisfied. For all your illustrious accomplishments, your moral cultivation has slipped."

"What have I done wrong?"

"At the beginning of your reign, you were afraid that your subordinates would not speak out, so you went out of your way to encourage them. Three years later, you could still be counted on to accept remonstrance with good grace. But in recent years, you are not happy to hear any criticism. Even if you listen to remonstrance, you look reluctant. In your heart you don't accept it."

Wei Zheng went on to cite a few examples to prove his point, and Taizong admitted they were true.

"Your subordinates are now afraid of you," Wei Zheng cautioned, "because you have become suspicious of their motives. You suspect that those who share the same view are cliquey. You treat frank advice as slander. So honest men can't speak their mind while sycophants are having a good time. As a result, I'm afraid your enterprise will end in failure."

"Nobody except you would tell me about it," replied Taizong. "I thought I hadn't changed much. Now I know I have some serious problems. I will definitely pay attention to them."

NOT ALIENATING FOLLOWERS

Wei Zheng cautioned Taizong again in a memorandum, "When a ruler is establishing a new regime, he is sincere to his followers. But once he has won, he becomes arrogant. When he treats people in good faith, they rally around him. When he becomes supercilious, even his own brother will be alienated. If he abuses his power and intimidates his subordinates, they will come up with various ways of countering him. Outwardly they may show respect, but inwardly they will feel resentful and will betray him in the end."

PAYING ATTENTION TO WARNING SIGNS

When Taizong had been on the throne for thirteen years, Wei Zheng noted some disturbing tendencies in him and wrote a memorandum to express his concern that if Taizong didn't change, his reign might not have a good ending.

"Your Majesty used to live a simple and frugal life," he pointed out. "Now you love luxury.

"Your Majesty used to cherish the people. Now you have imposed more taxes and corvée duties on them, saying it will be easier to govern them if the people are kept busy.

"Your Majesty used to like the company of virtuous men and keep villains at a distance. Now you keep the former at a respectful distance and surround yourself with sycophants.

"Your Majesty used to seek out talented men and was concerned when they were not given the opportunity to use their talents. Now you have become suspicious and capricious. A mere rumor can make you dismiss somebody who has served you for long years. Consequently, officials are more concerned about saving their skin than devoting themselves to work.

"Your Majesty used to respect your ministers and make everyone feel free to speak his mind. You maintained good communication with all your ministers. Now you have become aloof and inaccessible. When a minister reports to you, you don't have the patience to hear him out. And when you do listen, you often find fault with him. Your relationship with your subordinates is no longer harmonious.

"Your Majesty used to work hard and seldom took a rest. Now you do what you please. Your mind is not on your job but on how you can enjoy yourself. You are conceited, regarding yourself as a great ruler and looking down upon other great rulers in history."

Wei Zheng warned, "Your Majesty has laid a solid foundation for the dynasty for sure. But how long it will last depends largely on what you do from now on."

Upon reading the memorandum, Taizong said to his chief remonstrant, "Your points are well taken. I am deeply appreciative. You've made me aware of my mistakes. I'll do my best to rectify them. I've pasted your memorandum on the screen in my office so that I can read it often. I've also made a copy of it to be kept in the imperial library. A thousand years from now, when people read it, hopefully they will realize that ours is the right relationship between a ruler and a minister."

He awarded Wei Zheng a hundred ounces of gold and two fine horses.

AVOIDING COMPLACENCY

Heeding Wei's honest assessment, Taizong said, "Countless rulers in history failed because they became complacent. I've brought peace and prosperity to the realm; I've conquered the Turks and punished the Koreans. As China's prestige spreads, foreign countries send envoys to pay us tribute. But I'm afraid I may become conceited. So I continue to work hard, constantly reminding myself to be humble and to exercise self-discipline. If a minister gives me good advice, I treat him like a friend and a teacher. I hope I'll do better than my predecessors."

The Ruler's Guide

Taizong's struggle to not let self-satisfaction undermine his reign is poignantly relevant to our time.

After the demise of the Soviet Union and the end of the Cold War, the West indulged in a sense of complacency despite instability in many parts of the world. The US seemed to take its solitary superpower status for granted.

Reveling in their victory, many leaders in the West forgot the lessons of history. They failed to grasp the dynamics of a different world, didn't take new challenges seriously, and lacked a coherent strategy to cope with the new situation. Their vigilance relaxed, and their effort slackened because they thought they were in control.

The irony is that the West has found itself more vulnerable, more exposed to dangers now than even during the Cold War era. And because of a lapse in leadership, the West is now paying a much higher price to counter these dangers than it might otherwise have had to.

Taizong shows us what a wise leader must do when victory is won.

A wise leader doesn't rest on his laurels or indulge himself.

A wise leader understands that achieving victory is difficult but keeping it is even harder.

A wise leader knows that the seeds of decline are often planted in the peak of triumph.

A wise leader is alert to potential dangers even in times of peace.

A wise leader builds on his previous success to achieve new success.

A wise leader keeps the company of virtuous men and shuns sycophants.

A wise leader continues to encourage remonstrance.

A wise leader makes a point of studying history to learn its lessons.

11

On Parenting and Educating the Next Generation

All men are equal before God: wisdom, talents,
and virtue are the only difference between them.

—NAPOLÉON*

Taizong knew his children had gained their status the
easy way and he feared that they might lack the ability
and credibility to keep it. In particular, he worried that
the crown prince might lack the skill and strength to stand
on his own feet. For him, he did two things that proved
crucial: he lined up experienced ministers to assist the
future ruler, and he wrote an instruction manual for his
benefit. Judging by the longevity and reputation of the
Tang dynasty, Taizong's efforts in educating the younger
generation were richly rewarded.

* Napoléon (1769–1821) was the first emperor of France and one of
history's most celebrated military and political leaders.

TANG TAIZONG AND HIS ADVISERS' WORDS

CHOOSING TUTORS

Taizong told his advisers, "Highly intelligent men will not be affected by bad influences. But those of average intelligence are not so strong. Their moral character depends on what kind of education they receive. Choosing tutors for the princes is never easy. The tutors will have a tremendous impact on their pupils. I would like each of you to recommend a couple of upright and trustworthy men to be my sons' tutors. I'm growing old. If my children don't have a good education, the future of the dynasty will be in jeopardy."

PRACTICING VIRTUE

Taizong told his sons, "Heaven may endow a man with intellect, but he must study if he wants to accomplish something. When I was young, I was busy fighting enemies. Most of my time was spent on the battlefield. Now I have time to read, and I've learned a lot from books. I feel keenly about what the ancients said in regard to learning. 'Being ignorant is like facing a wall—you can't see anything.' As I recall what I did in the past, I realize that many things I did were wrong.

"It is your virtue, not your rank or wealth, that will establish you in the world. You are already well provided for. Wouldn't it be perfect if you cultivate your virtues? A gentleman may not always be a gentleman and a villain may not always be a villain. They can change. If you practice virtue, you'll be a gentleman; if you practice vice, you'll become a villain. If you don't study hard, don't exercise self-discipline, don't control your desires and emotions, you'll court disaster."

TAKING WARNING FROM HISTORY

Taizong said to Wei Zheng, "Few princes in history had a happy ending. This is because they grew up in the palace, wallowed in luxury and pleasure, and got into bad company." He asked his minister to write something for his children to study.

Wei Zheng compiled a book entitled *The Vices and Virtues of Princes in History*. In the introduction, he wrote:

"Throughout history, those princes who became good rulers had, along with their fathers, experienced hardships in the process of founding a new dynasty. Those who ended their life in disaster were born in the lap of luxury, brought up in peacetime, inherited a fortune, and were surrounded by pretty women and sycophantic ministers.

"History shows that the prosperity of a man comes from virtue and his destruction is the result of vice. Fortune or misfortune has no predetermined target. It all depends on what a man does. I list the vices and virtues of past princes in the book. Follow their good examples and avoid their mistakes, for that is the key to the longevity of the dynasty."

Taizong commended the book highly, telling his children to treat it as a moral compass to guide their lives.

LIMITING TERMS

Taizong said, "Officials working in the princes' quarters should not stay there too long, or they may develop overly close ties with the princes and have undue expectations. Limit their term to four years."

THE DOWNSIDE OF FAVORITISM

Taizong's favorite son was Tai, his second son. He showered gifts on him and granted him privileges. Minister Ma Zhou felt uneasy about this favoritism and wrote a memorandum.

"I know Your Majesty favors Tai over the other princes, but I'm concerned that Tai may become arrogant. I'm concerned about his future. During the Three Kingdoms period, Cao Cao, the ruler of Wei, was partial to his younger son. But when his elder son ascended the throne, his younger son was sent into exile and deprived of his freedom. Why? Because Cao Cao's favoritism had made his elder son jealous. Now, all your children are well provided for. Nobody needs any special favor. Please set some guidelines on their treatment."

Taizong thought it was good advice and awarded Ma Zhou generously.

TOUGH LOVE

Minister Chu Suiliang also voiced his disapproval of the emperor's favoritism.

"According to court etiquette," he advised Taizong, "the crown prince deserves higher honor than other princes because he is the future monarch. Even if Your Majesty likes Tai very much, your gifts should not exceed the level of what is appropriate. Otherwise, you will estrange the crown prince, cause confusion among your ministers, and give sycophants a chance to work on you. You may be too busy to make a correct decision on every issue, but it's my duty to speak out on this one. If Your Majesty really loves Tai, tell him to conduct himself properly, to practice loyalty, humility, and frugality and to cherish fraternal love. Inspire him with the teachings of the sages; then he'll grow up to be a worthy man."

Taizong accepted his minister's suggestions.

LATER GENERATIONS

"Why did disasters always strike in the later generations of a dynasty?" Taizong asked his ministers one day.

"Because the descendants of the founder," replied Prime Minister Fang Xuanling, "were born with silver spoons in their mouths. They didn't have any knowledge of the real world or any idea about running a country. It's no wonder they should have ended up in disaster."

"You put the blame on the rulers," said Taizong. "But

I think their ministers had to share the blame. They only cared about their self-interest. Their forefathers had rendered meritorious services. They occupied high offices because of their forefathers. However, they themselves were not particularly talented or virtuous. With an ignorant ruler and a bunch of useless ministers in charge, how could a country not get into trouble? Now your children will also obtain good appointments because of your position. I hope you'll draw a lesson from history and urge them to be conscientious officials. That will be good fortune for our country."

BOAT AND WATER

After appointing Crown Prince Zhi to be his heir, Taizong formed a team of senior ministers whose job it was to groom the future monarch and assist him in governing. He also took time to educate the prince himself.

He said to his advisers, "They say you should educate a child when it is still in its mother's womb. Well, I didn't have time for that. Now I teach him whenever I can."

He gave them an example. "When Zhi was having dinner, I asked him, 'Do you know anything about rice?'

"'No, I don't,' he answered.

"Then I said, 'Farming is hard work and timing is essential to farmers. Whatever you do, you must never interfere with their sowing and harvesting.'

"Seeing Zhi riding a horse, I asked, 'Do you know anything about horses?'

"'No, I don't.'

"Then I said, 'Horses are willing to work, but you must let them have some rest. If you don't overdrive them, you'll always have horses to ride.'

"Watching Zhi getting into a boat, I asked, 'Do you know anything about boats?'

"He said no. Then I told him, 'The king is like the boat, and the people are like the water. The water can lift the boat and also overturn it. Shouldn't you be very careful?'

"Seeing Zhi standing under a tree, I asked, 'Do you know anything about trees?'

"Again he said no and I said, 'This tree is not straight, but the carpenter can draw a line and cut it into straight pieces. Then the tree will be useful. A ruler may not be very capable, but if he listens to his ministers' good advice, he can still be a good ruler.'"

THE REAL WORLD

Taizong said to the tutors of the crown prince, "Talk to him about the real world and let him understand what the life of the common people is like. When I was eighteen, I worked among the masses of the common people and was familiar with their life. With all my knowledge of the real world and my experience of various hardships, I still made mistakes after I became emperor. Sometimes I didn't even realize my mistakes until somebody pointed them out. The crown prince has been living in the palace all his life; he has no idea about the outside world. Tell him not to indulge himself. Tell him why I encourage remonstrance. Be forthright with him if he does something wrong."

ROLE MODEL

Taizong told the crown prince to regard sage rulers in history as his role models.

"You should follow the examples of sage kings of the past, not me. I am not good enough. If you imitate superior men, you may get average results; if you imitate average men, you will end up worse than they were. Aim high. Don't follow my example.

"I have made many mistakes in my life, building luxurious palaces, acquiring exotic animals, hunting in distant lands, and giving the people trouble on my tours.

"But I have also done some good things, like improving the people's life, making the country rich and powerful, and so on. My merits probably outweigh my demerits. So the people put up with me.

"The foundation of our dynasty is sound, but I am ashamed to say that it is still far from perfect. Now you will inherit my fortune without having put in any effort. If you are a good ruler and serve the people wholeheartedly, you may be able to keep what you have. But if you become arrogant, indolent, self-indulgent, and extravagant, you will certainly get into trouble. Remember, it is easier to lose power than to gain it. It is easier to fail than to succeed. Therefore, you should cherish what you have and be very careful, should you not?"

WHAT TANG TAIZONG AND HIS ADVISERS TEACH US TODAY

Being responsible is a sign of maturity. When Taizong taught the crown prince to become responsible, he was helping him toward maturity. The metaphor of water and boat that he used to teach his son brings to mind the story of the sword of Damocles.

Dionysius was the king of Syracuse, the richest city in Sicily in the fourth century BC. He was wealthy, lived in a splendid palace, and had many servants.

When his friend Damocles complimented him on his riches and pleasure, Dionysius said, "If you think I'm so lucky, would you like to try out my life?"

Damocles readily agreed. So Dionysius ordered everything to be prepared for Damocles to experience what life as king was like. Damocles sat on the throne, was waited upon by the servants, and feasted on sumptuous food and wine amid beautiful flowers and scented candles.

He enjoyed all this immensely. Then he happened to raise his eyes, and saw a sword suspended from the ceiling by a hair above the throne. The smile faded from his lips and his face turned ashen.

"What is the matter?" asked the king.

"That sword! That sword!" cried Damocles.

"Yes," said the king, "I see the sword, and it may fall at any moment. I have it over my head all the time, and I always fear something may happen to snap the thread."

"I see," said Damocles. "I was mistaken. Your life is not so happy as it seems."

He begged to be excused and never wanted to change places with the king again.

Today, the expression "the sword of Damocles" is often used to mean impending danger. But the moral of the original story has been lost: if you aspire to something high, be it high power, high wealth, high honor, you must be prepared to live with the responsibilities and risks that come with it. It's easy to lose what you've gained if you don't keep making efforts to hold it.

12

On Being Well Remembered

A real man does what is right regardless of his self-interest; does what is sensible regardless of success or failure; and does what is good for future generations, not just for his own generation.

—HUANG ZONGXI*

Taizong was very conscious of the reputation he would leave behind. At his request, the Tang dynasty became the first to compile records of each emperor. Their every word and deed were noted down by scribes. Taizong generously rewarded his court historians. This must have had a favorable effect, for the account of his reign is among the most glorious in Chinese history.

---

* Huang Zongxi (1610–95) was a great Confucian philosopher and an Enlightenment thinker.

TANG TAIZONG AND HIS ADVISERS' WORDS

A GOOD ENDING

Taizong said to his ministers, "I often think about how I can have a good ending as well as a good beginning so that our dynasty will last many generations, so that hundreds of years from now when people read about the Tang dynasty, they will admire its power and glory."

FULL DISCLOSURE

Minister Chu Suiliang, who was also a court historian and remonstrant, kept a diary of Taizong's daily activities.

"What have you written down recently?" Taizong asked him one day.

"As a historian," replied Chu Suiliang, "I'm obliged to record whatever Your Majesty says and does, good or bad."

"Have you written down discreditable things about me?"

"Of course. My duty is to record facts — and facts only. I believe it is more important to fulfill my duty as a historian than my duty to Your Majesty as a subordinate."

"A ruler's faults are like the eclipses of the sun and the moon; everybody can see them," added Minister Liu Ji, another court historian. "Even if Minister Chu Suiliang didn't write them down, the people would remember."

"Well, I'll do three things," Taizong said. "First, I'll study the success and failure of past dynasties and draw lessons from them; second, I'll seek virtuous men to help me run the country; and third, I'll expel wicked men from my court. I hope history will be kind to me."

PREVIEW

As a rule, a living monarch was not supposed to read the account of his own rule. But Taizong couldn't suppress his curiosity about what the historians had written.

Zhu Zishe, a court remonstrant, tried to dissuade him from reading current accounts. He wrote the emperor a memorandum, saying, "Your Majesty is a wise ruler; it is fine for you to break the rule. But you would create a dangerous precedent. A future emperor may not be as wise as you are. If he is allowed to read what is written about him, he may become angry. He may punish or even kill the historians. If historians dare not write the truth, how can history be trusted? Your Majesty, please don't set such a precedent."

Taizong wasn't convinced. On another occasion, he asked Prime Minister Fang Xuanling, who supervised the writing of the current history of Tang, "Why is the reigning monarch not allowed to read what is written about him?"

"Because history must record the good and bad deeds of a ruler," Fang Xuanling explained. "Historians don't want the monarch to see what they have written for fear he may not like it."

"I disagree," said Taizong. "I would like to see what's been written about me. If it is favorable, of course no discussion is necessary. But if something bad is written down, surely it can serve as a warning for me."

He ordered Fang Xuanling to submit a copy of the most recent history, which covered the period from the rise of the emperor's father, Li Yuan, up to the fifteenth year of Taizong's reign. Taizong found the narration of his fratricide evasive.

"I did kill my brothers," he told Fang Xuanling. "It was for the good of the country. Do away with the verbiage and write a straightforward account of what happened. Do not hold back the facts."

Upon learning of this episode, Minister Wei Zheng praised Taizong. "The sovereign is the most powerful man in the country. He has nothing to fear except the historical record of his reign. The historical record has the function of chastising the bad ruler and encouraging the good ruler. If it is not truthful, it cannot serve later generations. Your Majesty did an honorable, fair-minded thing to tell the historians to set the record straight."

THE EMPEROR'S OWN WRITINGS

Deputy director of the Imperial Editorial Service Deng Shilong asked Taizong for permission to compile the emperor's writings into a collection as preceding rulers had done.

Taizong declined. "As emperor, what I said and did are all recorded in the imperial history. Even if I compose elegant poems and rhapsodies, I will only be held to ridicule by future generations if I fail to do a good job. I don't need any anthology. The most important thing for a ruler is what he does and what his character is like, not what literary works he writes."

SELF-ANALYSIS

"There are a few rulers in history," said Taizong to his ministers one day, "who restored peace and unified China, but none managed to conquer foreign barbarians. I'm not as capable as they were, yet my accomplishments have surpassed theirs. What do you think are the reasons?"

His ministers only sang his praises; no one offered a satisfactory explanation. Taizong then answered the question himself.

"I think there are five reasons. First, those rulers were jealous of people whose abilities exceeded their own, but I am not jealous. I am as pleased to discover other people's talents as if they were my own.

"Second, I understand that nobody is perfect. I overlook others' weaknesses and appreciate their strengths.

"Third, those rulers didn't know how to make use of human resources. They embraced talents but threw away lesser mortals. I respect the former but sympathize with the latter. I make use of both of them.

"Fourth, those rulers didn't like frankness. Some even killed those who dared to remonstrate. But I seek out honest men to serve in my court and I have never punished anyone for being outspoken.

"Finally, those rulers looked down upon foreigners, but I don't. I treat them the same way I treat Chinese. So the barbarians regard me as a father figure."

WHAT TANG TAIZONG AND HIS ADVISERS TEACH US TODAY

Plato said: "The first and the best victory is to conquer the self."

Taizong's life offers an instructive lesson in self-management without which his accomplishments would have been impossible.

It is not uncommon for a leader's personality to deteriorate. At the beginning of his career, the leader has a healthy ego; he is confident, assertive, and strong. He takes initiative and stands up for worthy causes, commanding the respect of those who turn to him for direction and inspiration.

Then he is tempted and starts to slip. He becomes arrogant, expansive, and belligerent. He loves adventures, wants to dominate each situation, and likes to impose his will on others, using threats and fear of reprisals to intimidate them into obedience, even relishing adversarial relationships.

Moving down the slope of virtue, he seeks to prevail whatever the cost. He becomes megalomaniacal, dictatorial, ruthless, and immoral. Increasingly reckless, he overextends himself and the resources at his disposal.

Having made many enemies, he becomes paranoid about his survival. He lives in constant insecurity, and his behavior turns destructive. In the end he is either toppled by his enemies or stopped by death.

A few notable rulers in history traveled this familiar path of disintegration with frightening consequences, among them Julius Caesar, Napoléon, and Saddam Hussein.

Taizong was quite the opposite. Early in his career, he threw himself into the struggle of founding the new dynasty. He was courageous and resourceful, often putting himself at risk for the sake of victory. Consequently he was recognized as an outstanding leader.

After he ascended the throne, he forgave his former enemy, recruited able and virtuous men, and upheld honesty in his government. He was magnanimous, empathetic, and forbearing. Even though he had lapses at times, he was able to reverse himself as soon as he realized his mistakes.

Internally, his triumph could be attributed to his self-knowledge and emotional intelligence, and externally, to the role played by his wife and loyal advisers, who would remonstrate whenever he veered away from the path of virtue and righteousness. The ignominious fall of Emperor Yang served as a constant reminder of what hell awaited if he slipped, and his own aspiration to make his dynasty a long-lasting one provided another positive impetus.

As a result, Taizong maintained a healthy state of mind throughout his life and avoided the pitfalls of his particular personality. Instead of moving downward, he moved upward, bringing out the best in himself and becoming, in the process, a very enlightened ruler.

Fittingly, his was one of the most spectacularly successful reigns in Chinese history.

II

THE AMAZING LIFE OF TANG TAIZONG

唐
太
宗
生
平

TANG TAIZONG'S personal name was Li Shimin, *"shi,"* meaning "the world," and *"min,"* "the people." When Li Shimin was a boy of four, a fortune-teller predicted that one day he would save the world and deliver the people from misery. Later, he became known as Tang Taizong, "Tang" being the name of the dynasty he helped found and "Taizong" his imperial title as emperor.

Born into the aristocratic Li family in Shaanxi Province in northwestern China, where his father was governor and a military commander serving the Sui dynasty, Li Shimin was of mixed Chinese and Turkic blood, for his paternal grandmother was a Turk. He was related to the royal family of Sui, and his family had a tradition of military service: both his grandfather and great-grandfather had also been high-ranking generals.

Bold, strong, and uninhibited, Li Shimin was not interested in scholarly pursuits but was keen on martial arts, archery, riding, and hunting. In a troubled time such skills were far more useful to an ambitious young man than book learning. Growing up in the waning years of the Sui dynasty, he witnessed the crumbling of that short-lived dynasty firsthand. Its decline was to have a major impact on him later, when he became emperor himself.

END OF THE SUI DYNASTY

The Sui dynasty (581–618) was one of the shortest dynasties in Chinese history, but also one of the most significant. Its founder, Emperor Wen, reunified China after nearly three hundred and sixty years of chaos and alien domination.

A conscientious monarch, Emperor Wen worked hard, lived frugally, and built a stable and prosperous country. But his son and successor, Emperor Yang, was one of history's most notorious rulers—ambitious, cruel, egomaniacal, and callous to the suffering of the people.

The first thing Emperor Yang did after succeeding his father was to build another capital in Luoyang, because a fortune-teller told him that the existing capital, Chang'an (the present-day Xi'an), was an unlucky location for him. Two million laborers were conscripted to construct magnificent palaces and a huge pleasure park for him. The entire project was finished within a year under intense pressure. By then four out of every ten laborers had died from exhaustion.

Hardly had the new capital been completed when the emperor embarked on an even more ambitious project— the digging of a canal system, the Grand Canal, to link the north and south of China. More than three million laborers were conscripted. Because there were not enough men, a large number of women were used. During the six-year construction, nearly half of the laborers lost their lives.

Emperor Yang loved traveling. He was on the move every year during his fourteen-year reign, and his trips imposed an intolerable burden on the people. If he traveled by water, tens of thousands of men had to be hired to pull his extravagant fleet along rivers and canals. If he traveled on land, tree-lined boulevards and imperial dwelling places had to be built and large numbers of horses and carriages had to be prepared. Wherever his entourage went, relentless requisitions were made on the local populace in the form of rare delicacies and luxury goods for imperial consumption.

While the masses were groaning under his oppression, the emperor delighted in the company of hundreds of beautiful women in his harem. As he took his pleasure with them, mirrors were hung on the walls of his bedchamber so he could feast his eyes on the carnal scenes. He particularly liked to tie a virgin's hands and feet on a "virgin cart" while deflowering her.

Before the people could recover from the domestic burdens, the emperor launched a war against the Korean kingdom of Koguryo because he suspected Koguryo of forming a secret alliance with the Turks against China. Special war taxes were levied, new soldiers were recruited, and corvée labor was employed to construct war vehicles and navy vessels. Since shipbuilders had to stand in the water day and night, the lower bodies of many decomposed; many also died of overwork or disease. Emperor Yang led three expeditions; all ended in disaster, with the loss of hundreds of thousands of lives.

While Yang was waging campaigns in Korea, a rebellion broke out at home. It soon turned into a tidal wave of uprisings sweeping over the entire realm. Yang rushed back to China but was unable to quell the popular revolts. In the end even his own generals mutinied and the emperor was strangled to death in his palace.

ROAD TO POWER

Many ambitious men rose to contend for the title of emperor. Taizong's father, Li Yuan, was one of them. It wasn't until three years later, after many hard-fought battles, that the house of Tang—named after Li Yuan's hereditary fief— emerged victorious.

During this period, Shimin, his second son, proved himself to be a valiant fighter, a superb commander, and a gifted strategist who carried out his assignments with distinction, earning his troops' fierce loyalty and his enemies' respect. Shimin's military feats played a crucial role in solidifying the power of Tang. Consequently, Li Yuan appointed him commander in chief of the army. A fearless warrior, Shimin openly admitted that he'd personally slain nearly a thousand men in various battles.

Li Yuan had twenty-two sons and nineteen daughters. In accordance with imperial tradition, he named his eldest son crown prince. But Shimin's soaring reputation made his brother, whose own military merits were far from illustrious, feel ill at ease. The court ministers were divided into those who were loyal to the crown prince and those who considered Shimin the more deserving to succeed to the throne.

Shimin didn't openly proclaim his aspiration but began preparing himself for the throne early on by recruiting an impressive array of political and literary talents as his think tank. After finishing a day's work, he would study the Confucian classics, history, and literature under the tutelage of well-known scholars and discuss with them current affairs and policy matters.

The sibling rivalry culminated in a fratricide in 626, when Shimin and his men murdered the crown prince and another brother in an ambush and forced Li Yuan to relinquish power. Shimin became the second Tang emperor and took the imperial title of Taizong. His reign was officially inaugurated in 627 when he was twenty-eight, or twenty-nine according to Chinese reckoning, which defines a child as one year old at birth.

TAIZONG AND HIS ADVISERS

A charismatic ruler, Taizong went about his work with boundless energy and enthusiasm, and he demanded equal exertion from his officials. He consulted his gifted advisers at daily meetings, drawing on their knowledge and experience to run the government. His senior ministers slept in shifts so that he could summon them at any time, day or night, to discuss the affairs of the empire.

A man of sharp intellect, Taizong possessed shrewd judgment and knew how to use people's strengths and avoid their weaknesses. He wouldn't hesitate to hire a former enemy if the man had talent and integrity. He pardoned most of the followers of the crown prince on account of their loyalty to their master. For example, General Yuchi had been a rebel commander and Defense Minister Li Jing had been a high-ranking Sui general. Senior Minister Wang Gui had been an adviser to the crown prince. Senior Minister and Chief Remonstrant Wei Zheng, another senior adviser to his brother, had been a hated figure in Taizong's camp.

"Why did you set my brother against me?" demanded Taizong as Wei Zheng was brought before him.

"If the crown prince had listened to my advice, he would never have come to such an end," Wei Zheng replied calmly.

Taizong had long heard of the man's talent, and his candor impressed him. He asked Wei Zheng to be one of his advisers.

"Wei Zheng should be executed," someone suggested.

"No. Wei Zheng was loyal to his master," Taizong replied. "I can trust him. It is those who betrayed their master in difficulty who deserve to die."

In an attempt to remove the stigma of slaying his brothers, Taizong conferred noble titles on them posthumously and had them reburied at a grand ceremony attended by their former subordinates. This conciliatory gesture made these people feel at ease working for the new ruler.

Assembled around Taizong was a range of confidants, advisers, and supporters, each with unique strengths. They complemented one another, forming a strong management team. For example, Prime Minister Fang Xuanling was detail-oriented and good at planning; his colleague Vice Prime Minister Du Ruhui was quick, decisive, and resourceful. The two men made a perfect partnership.

Most of Taizong's advisers were his elders. Wei Zheng and Du Ruhui were his seniors by nineteen years, Fang Xuanling by twenty-one years, Li Jing by twenty-seven years, and Wang Gui by twenty-eight years.

Taizong once asked Senior Minister Wang Gui to give an appraisal of his colleagues. "I'm not as assiduous as Fang Xuanling," replied Wang Gui, "who puts work above everything else. I'm not as impassioned as Wei Zheng when I remonstrate; not as all-around as Li Jing, who has the caliber of a prime minister and a general; neither am I as good as Wen Yanbo, who knows how to convey Your Majesty's ideas clearly, or as good as Dai Zhou, who handles matters big and small equally well. But I have my own strength. I have a strong sense of justice. I promote the virtuous and crack down on the wicked without reserve."

Taizong and his other ministers thought it was a fair assessment.

LISTENING TO REMONSTRANCE

What set Taizong apart from most emperors was his willingness to listen to different opinions and heed remonstrances. Remonstrance was the time-honored practice in ancient China of officials criticizing the ruler's policy and personal behavior and advising him on ways to improve his government. Taizong went out of his way to encourage his ministers to criticize him for his mistakes. They could either speak to him face-to-face or write to him.

Stalwart and dashing, Taizong cut an intimidating figure at court. He had an imperial bearing. When provoked, his face would change color and strike fear into those around him. After Wei Zheng cautioned him about it, Taizong said to his ministers: "If I want to see myself, I need a mirror. If I want to know my faults, I need loyal ministers. Please speak out freely about my faults. I promise I won't become angry."

True to his words, he was exceedingly gentle with his subordinates. He might not like what he had heard but nevertheless kept a pleasant countenance. He was willing to admit his mistakes in public and praise those who pointed them out. Time and again, he offered monetary rewards to those who remonstrated with him.

As a result, not only senior ministers but petty officials, and even court ladies, came forward to offer suggestions and remonstrances. When their memorandums became too numerous, Taizong had them posted on the walls of his living quarters so that he could read them after work.

CHIEF REMONSTRANT WEI ZHENG

The most outspoken adviser was the Confucian moralist Senior Minister and Chief Remonstrant Wei Zheng, who'd earned Taizong's trust and respect with his candor, loyalty, fearlessness, and profound knowledge.

In the first three years of Taizong's reign, Wei Zheng made more than two hundred suggestions, asking Taizong to conduct himself and his policies in accordance with Confucian principles of virtue and benevolence.

Wei Zheng skillfully used extravagant praise, subtle hints, plain ridicule, and blunt attack, laced with historical anecdotes and classical allusions, as tactics for his remonstration. As a result his remarks carried irresistible power. The subjects of his remonstrances were extensive: the inconsistencies in Taizong's taxation policy, his ill-conceived proposal of awarding hereditary fiefs to his children, his interest in the fair sex and creature comforts, his lack of humility, his vanity, and so on.

Some of Wei Zheng's comments, though scathingly critical, were voiced in front of other ministers. Taizong had to accept his criticism with as much grace as he could muster. Sometimes Wei Zheng's words were too caustic and roused Taizong to anger. Most ministers were frightened, but Wei Zheng would keep his composure, totally unawed and uncompromising. In fact, it was the young emperor who was a little afraid of the avuncular remonstrant.

Taizong loved birds. One day he was playing with a lovely sparrow when Wei Zheng came to see him. Afraid that Wei Zheng might scold him for playing during working hours, Taizong hid the bird inside the sleeve of his robe. Wei Zheng pretended not to notice and stayed on to discuss various business matters for so long that by the time he left, the bird had already been smothered to death.

A senior minister was not impressed. "Wei Zheng talks

too much," he said, "harping on the same tune until Your Majesty listens to him. He treats you like a child."

"I've got battlefield experience," said Taizong, "but know little about running the government. I value Wei Zheng's advice. He is helping me make fewer mistakes and is not afraid of offending me. I hope all of you will follow his example."

But Wei Zheng apparently pushed the emperor to the limit one day. Taizong was livid with anger when he came home in the evening.

"I'm going to kill that boor," he grumbled.

"Who are you talking about?" asked Empress Zhangsun.

"Wei Zheng! I raised him from the dust. But he dares to insult me before the entire court. I'll never be my own master as long as he is around."

The empress withdrew to her bedroom. Moments later, she came out in her regal costume and kowtowed to her husband, who stared at her in puzzlement.

"I heard that an enlightened ruler is served by faithful and upright ministers," she said. "You've just told me Wei Zheng is such a man. That means you are an enlightened ruler. I want to congratulate you."

She went on to explain, "Even as your wife, I have to watch out for your mood when I talk. I don't want to provoke your anger. But Wei Zheng has the courage to tell you the truth even when he knows the truth may displease you."

Instantly, she turned Taizong's anger into joy. So he let Wei Zheng continue to "scrape scales off the dragon" with impunity, this being a Chinese metaphor for directly criticizing the ruler. He was moved by Wei Zheng's loyalty and genuine concern for the well-being and longevity of the dynasty.

He urged his senior ministers to accept remonstrances as he did. A titled position—the remonstrant—was created. Thirty-six remonstrants would sit in various court meetings and voice their opinions.

PROSPERITY AT HOME

Along with his ministers, Taizong devoted major efforts to economic reconstruction. He thought the country was like a patient who needed recuperation after more than ten years of civil war and political instability.

Tang China was an agrarian economy. But there was a labor shortage. War and war-related migration had caused the population to drop to about twelve million—less than a third of what it had been in the Sui dynasty. One of the first decrees Taizong issued was that men had to get married by twenty and women by fifteen, while widows and widowers were encouraged to remarry. Wealthy people were urged to provide money for their poor relatives and neighbors to enable them to afford marriage. An important criterion for evaluating local officials was the number of marriages that took place in their localities.

Taizong released thousands of palace maids, not only to reduce expenditure but to allow them to marry. He also requested that the Turks and other foreign states allow the two million Chinese who'd fled to their lands during the warring years to come home.

Taizong renewed an ancient rite in which he, the Son of Heaven, officially started the plowing season by tilling a field himself. His message was this: farming was now the nation's priority. To promote farming, taxes and corvée duties were kept low. A male over eighteen years of age would be given a hundred *mu* (approximately fourteen acres) of land, of which twenty *mu* would become his permanent property and eighty *mu* had to be returned to the state upon his death. In return, he only had to pay a tax of less than 3 percent on his income in the form of grain and cloth plus perform twenty days' corvée duty a year. In the event of natural disasters, taxes were reduced or exempted.

Irrigation works were carried out throughout the country. In some regions, there was not enough arable land. So Taizong encouraged migration by offering tax exemption as an incentive to those who would leave home to open up virgin soil in faraway places.

In a few years, the economy recovered; the war-ravaged country was on its way to prosperity.

RECRUITING TALENTS

Taizong was eager to recruit "the worthy" to work in his government. The criteria for "worthiness" were erudition, moral integrity, and filial piety. His zeal for education was prompted by a desire to have a pool of talented individuals from which he could choose, particularly those who were dedicated to the Confucian values of loyalty to the ruler and duty to the people.

Thousands of students and scholars swarmed into Chang'an each year to sit for imperial examinations. All candidates, including many foreign students, were on an equal footing, regardless of race, family background, or hereditary privileges.

Taizong instructed Prime Minister Fang Xuanling to appoint to office those who possessed both talents *and* virtues, not only those with specialized skills.

For a long time, appointments in the central government had been deemed more prestigious than those in the provinces. Provincial posts had become dumping grounds for those officials who'd performed poorly in the central government.

Taizong felt sure that provincial officials would be perceived by local people as the emperor's deputies. So he sent out commissioners to scrutinize their conduct and job performance.

He wrote the names of these provincial officials on the screens in his room and kept a record of their performances. Their promotions and demotions were determined by the merits and demerits he recorded. The bases for promotion were talent, honesty, prudence, diligence, and fair-mindedness.

PROMOTION OF EDUCATION

Taizong was convinced that selection for the civil service was vital to good government and even the survival of the dynasty. Selection through means of examination embodied the Confucian ideal of equal opportunity in education for all. Taizong ordered more examinations to be held each year and more schools to be built, not only in the capital but also in the provinces, counties, and villages. Qualifications for teachers were standardized.

Confucian doctrine served as a guide in formulating the policies of Taizong's government, and temples to Confucius were erected all over the country. Since the Han dynasty, there had been many different versions and confusing interpretations of Confucian classics. Taizong appointed a renowned scholar to preside over the compilation of an authorized version, which was to be used by all schools and serve as the basis for imperial examinations.

From time to time, Taizong went to the imperial university to listen to the lectures, often generously rewarding good lecturers. One day he visited there dressed in plain clothes. A large number of candidates lined up outside the entrance where a bulletin board listed the names of those who'd passed the examination.

It was a gratifying scene. "How nice it is to have all the talents under heaven come within my reach!" Taizong exclaimed.

This merit-based selection system has become part of the Chinese tradition and the cornerstone of civil service recruitment policy in China.

LEGAL REFORM

Taizong firmly subscribed to the Confucian view that it is virtues, not harsh laws, that make a good society. During the early years of his reign, the criminal code was substantially revised and simplified from more than two thousand clauses to seven hundred, and harsh punishments were either abolished or reduced for many penal offenses. Officers who tortured prisoners to death would be charged with manslaughter.

The Tang court system had three levels: the county court, the provincial court, and the supreme court. Death penalties had to be approved by the supreme court and the emperor himself.

Twice Taizong ordered the execution of some officials, and twice he regretted his decision, only to find it was too late to rescind the order. To avoid miscarriages of justice, he ordered that even if the death penalty was approved, it had to be reviewed three times by different departments before being carried out. As a result, the number of death-row convicts declined significantly.

While Taizong encouraged honest criticism, he hated slanderers. An anti-false-accusation law was devised to deal with such people. The accuser would be punished according to the nature of his false accusation. For example, a man accused Wei Zheng of treason, a capital crime. Since his charge was absolutely unfounded, the man was beheaded.

Another general, who was an old associate of Taizong, accused Defense Minister Li Jing of plotting a rebellion, a crime punishable by death. But investigation proved Li Jing innocent. According to the law, the accuser faced the death penalty. Taizong commuted the death penalty to exile on account of the man's earlier meritorious services but rejected his plea for more lenient treatment.

Having spent his formative years in the military, Taizong valued loyalty. He decreed that a servant who informed on his master would be put to death.

TACKLING CORRUPTION

Taizong abhorred corruption. Officials convicted of accepting bribes would be punished. Those convicted of serious corruption would be executed. On the day of execution, government officials were requested to witness the execution so that they might think twice before they were tempted to accept bribes.

The law prohibited prefectural and county officials from serving in their native places for fear that their relatives and friends might try to seek favor from them. Officials were prohibited from taking their parents or children over fifteen with them to their posts so as to prevent their families from becoming channels of bribery and favoritism. And officials couldn't serve in places where they'd previously held positions for fear that they might be influenced by local interests. The term of office was limited to four years.

Dang Renhong, governor of Guangdong, an old associate of Taizong's, was found guilty of taking bribes and levying taxes without authority. He was sentenced to death. But considering the man's advanced age and meritorious services, Taizong decided just to dismiss him from office. Knowing such leniency would be at odds with the law, the emperor started a three-day fast as a gesture to ask Heaven to forgive him his merciful act.

Prime Minister Fang Xuanling admonished him to stop fasting. "As emperor, you have the power to grant him clemency. You are not doing it out of selfish motives. Why should you ask Heaven for forgiveness?"

Taizong replied, "The law is not my law but the law of the land." He then issued a mea culpa apologizing for pardoning his old colleague.

The historian Wu Jing wrote a glowing passage about life under Taizong's reign:

> For fear of the emperor, officials were honest and cautious in exercising their power; nobles and local elite restrained themselves, not daring to encroach upon the rights of the common people.
>
> Merchants were not robbed on their trips. The prisons were empty. Horses and cattle roamed the open country. Doors did not need to be locked. There were bumper harvests year after year. Travelers from the capital to the east coast did not need to carry provisions on their way. They would be generously supplied and well treated, sometimes even presented with gifts when they departed. There had been nothing like this since ancient times.

CONQUEST OF THE TURKS

Externally, Taizong's most important victory was the conquest of the Turks. Descended from the ancient Huns, the Turks were a nomadic tribe living in Mongolia at the time. They'd been a constant threat to China's northern borders. After being defeated by Emperor Wen of the Sui dynasty, they were divided into Eastern and Western Turks. During the years of China's civil war preceding Taizong's reign, they grew powerful again.

Before launching his bid for power, Taizong's father had to negotiate peace with the Eastern Turks by pledging to be a Turkic vassal. After the founding of the Tang dynasty, the Turks kept demanding more and more tribute from the new regime. The Tang court had to put up with their insolent envoys while Turkic troops repeatedly raided Chinese border areas, killing, looting, and making Chinese captives their slaves.

Shortly after Taizong succeeded to the throne, the Eastern Turks invaded China and came within twelve miles of the Tang capital, Chang'an. Taizong held a face-to-face meeting with the khan, sovereign of the Turks. After Taizong agreed to give them a large amount of gold, silver, and silk, the Turks signed a peace treaty and withdrew.

Vowing to wipe out the humiliation, Taizong embarked on a large-scale military buildup. In 630, the Chinese army launched surprise attacks against the Turks on three fronts simultaneously. The expedition was a resounding success. The Turkic forces were crushed. The khan was taken prisoner and brought to Chang'an. He was publicly denounced by Taizong but allowed to live.

Taizong permitted many surrendered Turks to resettle in China in the hope that if the nomads took up agriculture and were influenced by Chinese culture, they'd cease to be a threat. Unlike other Chinese emperors, who tended to discriminate against foreigners, Taizong let the Turks work in his government. More than a hundred Turkic noblemen joined the Tang army as officers and took an active part in Taizong's expeditions in Central Asia and Korea, during which several ranking Turkic generals rendered outstanding services.

The khan was appointed as a senior general, but it was only a nominal post. A virtual captive, he was depressed, he wept often, and his health deteriorated. Once the khan was ordered by Taizong's father to dance at a banquet to entertain the banqueters. He felt so humiliated that he died shortly afterward.

In 639, an assassination attempt was made on Taizong by a half brother of the khan, who was a junior officer in the Tang army. He and a handful of accomplices were overpowered by the palace guards and publicly beheaded. After the incident, all Turks, except for a few trusted senior officers, were required to leave China to settle in Mongolia.

SILK ROAD

At the time, the vast region now called the Chinese provinces of Xinjiang and Qinghai was divided into a number of tribal kingdoms, some allying with the Western Turks. Their territories covered what was known as the Silk Road, an important route along which merchants from the Roman Empire, Persia, and Central Asia traveled to China. But this route was often blocked by those tribes. Merchants were detained; their wares were confiscated; Chinese borders were frequently invaded by marauders. Having dealt with the problem of the Eastern Turks, Taizong decided to remove the threat on the Silk Road once and for all.

Between 635 and 648, Chinese troops successively conquered Tuyuhun, Gaochang (Karakhoja), Yanchi (Karashahr), Xueyantuo (Syr Tardush), and Qiuzi (Kucha), making them China's vassals. The Western Turks were compelled to offer their submission. As a result, China took control of the vast area stretching from Dunhuang in modern Gansu to the western borders of the Tarim Basin in Xinjiang.

Trade between China and Central Asia flourished. Silk, tea, medicine, ceramics, handicrafts, paper, and farm tools were exported, while jade, fur, horses, camels, lions, and cotton were imported.

At the request of various khanates in Central Asia, Taizong assumed the imposing title of "Heavenly Khan"—the suzerain of all Turks. In this capacity, he played the role of an arbiter for tribal khanates in Central Asia. When they had a dispute about horse-breeding territories, for instance, they came to Taizong, whose arbitration was thought to be fair by all parties. Every New Year, chiefs and noblemen from various tribes came to China to pay their respects. A meeting with Taizong was deemed a great honor.

The only blemish on Taizong's shining military record was the failure of his war against the Korean kingdom of Koguryo, which had been meant to punish the country for invading a Chinese vassal state. But this didn't affect China's stature as a great world power.

WEDLOCK DIPLOMACY AND TIBETAN TIES

Wedlock diplomacy had a long history in China. Typically, a Chinese princess, a highly desirable status symbol, would be married to the king of some nomadic kingdom that bordered on China. It was a way of bringing peace to the border when China was relatively weak.

Taizong practiced wedlock diplomacy at a time when China was strong, because he felt that if a marital tie could turn foes into friends, it was worth the sacrifice of a Chinese princess. Compared with the cost of a wedding, the cost of war was too high. To conquer an enemy through marriage was undoubtedly better than to conquer it through war, for the children born of such a marriage would likely remain friendly to China.

Thus, a number of Tang princesses were married off to foreign kings and noblemen. The most notable union was the marriage between Princess Wencheng, Taizong's adopted daughter, and Songtsen Gampo, the Tibetan king.

In 641, a large Chinese convoy accompanied the princess to Tibet, bringing with them Chinese foodstuffs, textiles, medicine, plants, grain, and vegetable seeds, as well as Chinese artisans, craftsmen, workers, farmers, and builders.

Tibetans traditionally lived in felt tents, but now they moved into houses after learning building techniques from the Chinese. They'd formerly worn furs, but now they put on silk garments and learned to weave. They'd never used a calendar, but now they adopted the lunar calendar, a boon to their farmers and herdsmen. The Chinese also instructed Tibetans in pottery, brewing, grain milling, papermaking, and the manufacture of farm tools. The princess brought with her a band of musicians and more than fifty musical instruments. They were much cherished by Tibetans.

Since Tibetans lacked a standard written language, Princess Wencheng persuaded her husband to send students to India to study Sanskrit and the ancient Khotan (Yudian) language with a view to developing a Tibetan alphabet and grammar from an Indian prototype.

The princess was a devout Buddhist. Under her influence, the Tibetan king embraced Buddhism. Today, a gilded and bejeweled statue of Buddha, a gift brought by the princess as her dowry, is still enshrined in the splendid Jokhang Temple in Lhasa, the capital of Tibet.

Contact with the Tibetans led to the introduction of Tibetan horse-breeding skill and Tibetan handicraft into China. When polo was introduced from Tibet, it became a popular sport in the Tang court.

RELIGIOUS TOLERANCE

Trade thrived along the Silk Road to Central Asia, Persia, and Europe and along the sea route to Southeast Asia. Arabs, Jews, and Persians came to settle in China, bringing with them Islam, Christianity, Judaism, and Zoroastrianism.

Taizong was tolerant of religion. In 635, he greeted a Nestorian bishop from Persia, the first Christian missionary to come to China, and granted him permission to use the facilities of the imperial library to translate the Holy Bible. He also issued a decree that provided for the building of the first church in China, where the bishop preached. The Christian faith and Jesus were introduced to the Chinese for the first time. The modern Chinese hymnal has a hymn, "Gloria in Excelsis," that dates back to the Tang dynasty.

Taizong said that no religion held a monopoly on truth since they all claimed to be saving people. Emotionally, however, he was closer to Taoism. He claimed that the founder of Taoism, Lao Tzu, whose family name was Li, was his ancestor. He considered Taoism to be indigenous to China while Buddhism, which was very popular in China, was alien.

"The problem with Buddhism," Taizong commented, "is that while the believer is not sure of his future happiness, he is trapped by what he allegedly did in his previous life."

His disapproving attitude didn't prevent him from being interested in the adventures of a great Buddhist pilgrim named Xuanzang who, surmounting tremendous dangers and difficulties, traversed ten thousand miles to India to study Buddhist doctrine.

Xuanzang spent nineteen years abroad and returned to China in 645 to a hero's welcome, bringing back more than six hundred Buddhist books. He wrote a book about his journey to what are today India, Pakistan, Bangladesh, Sri Lanka, Nepal, Afghanistan, and numerous other places.

His legendary adventures are immortalized in the famous Ming novel *Journey to the West*.

Taizong met him and was impressed by the man's erudition and personality. Subsequently, he wrote a flattering foreword to the Chinese version of Buddhist sutras translated by Xuanzang. And his views on Buddhism became more favorable.

Meanwhile, Islam gained wide acceptance in China's northwestern border regions, surviving energetically to this day.

HOBBIES

Strong and energetic, Taizong enjoyed outdoor activities. He was fond of archery and was one of the best marksmen of his time. The bow he used was twice the normal size and strong enough to shoot through an iron door. His marksmanship saved his life many times on the battlefield.

He had a passion for horses, and his horsemanship was as good as his marksmanship. He commissioned an artist to carve his six favorite war stallions in bas-relief on stone and had them placed in his tomb. Their vivid images have been preserved to this day.

Hunting was his favorite sport, but the kind of hunting Taizong engaged in was an expensive proposition. It resembled military exercises in which soldiers surrounded a wide area of country and drove the game to the center, where hunters were waiting.

During the hunting excursion, Taizong and his companions, all excellent archers and swordsmen in colorful hunting outfits and accompanied by dogs and falcons, would go out early in the morning on horses draped in tiger skin and return late at night. Taizong would fight with wild animals at close range just for the thrill of fighting.

One day Taizong was attacked by a pack of wild boars. He shot dead four, but one nearly knocked over his horse. An aide jumped off his horse to come to his rescue but lost his own weapon and had to fight barehanded. It was Taizong who finally killed the boar with his sword.

"Why were you so scared?" he said, laughing at the man. "Did you see how I fight?"

The aide was not amused, though. "Your Majesty is the ruler of the country. Why did you risk your life to fight a beast? To show off your bravery?"

The man apparently didn't appreciate Taizong's penchant for hunting. In fact, Taizong wrote quite a few poems about his love for hunting, for horses, and for archery. Other topics touched on in his more than one hundred poems were the city scenes of Chang'an, natural beauty, court occasions, and philosophical reflections.

Taizong was also musically inclined. The music and dance performed at ancestral worship ceremonies, state banquets, and New Year celebrations symbolized the cultural and artistic achievements of the dynasty. According to Chinese tradition, each dynasty would compose its own music after it was founded. Taizong was closely involved in creating the Tang music, which incorporated a variety of Chinese and foreign musical elements.

He choreographed an elaborate court dance, eulogizing Tang's military successes. It was performed regularly at palace dinner parties. A minister proposed that scenes of rebel leaders being captured be added to the dance. Taizong rejected the idea, saying that since quite a few of his former enemies were serving in his court, doing so would hurt their feelings. It would have the opposite effect of what dance and music were supposed to engender.

Taizong was also adept at calligraphy, which was considered a fine art in China. A good hand was a mark of social distinction and scholarship. Calligraphy by grand masters was earnestly copied and studied. Pieces of their handwriting were treasured works of art and Taizong was an ardent collector.

EMPRESS ZHANGSUN

Taizong had a wife, Empress Zhangsun, and seven concubines, who bore him fourteen sons and twenty-one daughters. He loved his wife dearly. They were married when he was fifteen and she was twelve. The empress was the daughter of a distinguished Sui general and was well educated, but when her husband asked her opinion on affairs of state, she'd say it was inappropriate for her to get involved in politics.

Her brother Zhangsun Wuji was Taizong's boyhood friend and had played a major role in Taizong's rise to power. When Wuji was appointed prime minister, the empress persuaded him to resign because she was concerned about nepotism.

She told Taizong, "Because of my marriage, many of my relatives are occupying high positions that they don't deserve. Their positions are precarious. I hope you will not appoint any more of them for their own sakes."

The empress was kind to all those in the palace's employ. If she believed her husband had punished a eunuch or a maid without a good reason, she'd pretend to be as angry as he was and offer to look into the person's offenses. She'd wait until her husband had calmed down before interceding on the person's behalf, making sure there was no injustice done in her household.

She compiled a collection of stories about well-known virtuous women and well-known villainous women in history for all the court ladies to read.

When she fell seriously ill, her son suggested that she let Taizong order a general amnesty in the hope that a gesture of clemency might move the gods to save her, but the empress refused.

"Life and death are determined by fate, which human beings cannot change," she said. "If doing good brings fortune, I've never done anything wrong in my life. If not, what's the use of praying to gods? An amnesty is a matter of grave consequence. It should not be trifled with. Don't do it for my sake."

To make a stand against the prevalent practice of expensive funerals among both the upper class and the common people, the empress told Taizong on her deathbed, "I've done very little for the country. Please don't waste money to build a mausoleum for me. Just bury me in the mountain.

No need to call back the children to the capital. It would only make me upset to see them crying."

When she died at the age of thirty-five, Taizong's grief knew no bounds. To comply with her wish, no treasure was buried in her tomb; the only objects there were some human figures and horses made of wood and ceramics.

"I hope she won't be disturbed," remarked Taizong. "There's no treasure inside. Grave robbers ought to spare her tomb. All my family should be buried this way."

AN ENLIGHTENED RULER

Taizong's regnal years were called Zhenguan, meaning "true vision"—the vision of a great empire under a wise ruler. Taizong wanted history to remember the grandeur and splendor of his dynasty. To a large extent, he was successful. When he died in 649, Taizong had laid down the foundation of a dynasty that was to last nearly three hundred years.

Tang China was confident, vibrant, and open to new ideas and new immigrants. The wealth of Tang China attracted visitors from far and near. The poetry, painting, and architecture of Tang China were the admiration of the world.

The capital, Chang'an, was the world's most open and cosmopolitan city in the seventh century. It was the center of art, literature, fashion, and advanced learning in Asia. The city's most imposing feature was the imperial palace with its halls, towers, gardens, pavilions, and compounds.

The streets were bustling; the marketplaces were crowded. Envoys from Persia, Japan, and India flocked to pay their respects. Merchants from the West, Buddhist monks from India, Nestorian priests from Syria, and Taoist magicians rubbed shoulders with one another.

Tang China recruited talents from all over the world. Many generals and officials were of non-Chinese origin. Tang culture heavily influenced those of Korea, Japan, and Vietnam. Never since the mighty Han dynasty had China attained such power and prestige.

During the Tang period, Chinese started traveling and emigrating overseas. They identified themselves as the "people of Tang," and if they settled down in a place, they called their enclave the "town of Tang." To this day Chinese in the West still refer to Chinatown, whether it is the Chinatown in New York or the Chinatown in London, as the "town of Tang," and Chinese in Southeast Asia refer to themselves as the "people of Tang."

One year before his death, Taizong summed up his life in the following words.

> Reading history, I discovered all the founding emperors of new dynasties came to power only after the age of forty, except Emperor Guangwu of the Han dynasty, who was thirty-three when he ascended the throne. I was an army commander at eighteen. I defeated all the rebel forces at twenty-four and became emperor at twenty-nine. I was

quite young when I joined the army. I didn't have much time to study. Therefore, after becoming emperor, I made an effort to read whenever I was free.

I've learned the principles of good governance and put them into practice. Our country was going downhill, but it is now in good shape. Foreign barbarians used to invade China, but they are now our vassals. I'm very lucky, for I've done better than many rulers in history. I want to make sure that my rule has a good beginning and a good ending.

His self-appraisal is not exactly modest but by and large fair. Taizong wanted history to remember him as a forceful and decisive yet wise and benevolent monarch. Throughout his career, he retained the qualities that singled him out as an enlightened ruler—he was reflective, self-conscious, open-minded, and receptive to criticism.

His willingness to listen to remonstrance stemmed from his vivid memory of Emperor Yang's misrule and subsequent downfall, from his wish to be a brilliant ruler as well as a superior military leader, and from his desire to leave a good name in history's annals, a desire not unrelated to his fratricidal act.

Today, he is revered as among the greatest emperors of China. As a wise and rational monarch, he is a role model for all rulers. And his dynasty is recognized as one of the most glorious eras in Chinese history.

Author's Note

This book is the result of years of research as well as the study of numerous Chinese classics. My primary source was *The Zhenguan Executive Guide* (*Zhenguan Zhengyao*), compiled by Wu Jing (670–749).

Other significant source materials are as follows:

- *Tang Taizong and General Li Jing on the Art of War*, compiled by Du You (735–812)
- *Guide for the Emperor* (*Difan*) by Tang Taizong
- *A Comprehensive Mirror for Rulers* (*Zizhi Tongjian*) by Sima Guang (1019–86) et al.
- *History of the Sui* by Wei Zheng (580–643) et al.
- *Old History of the Tang* by Liu Xu (870–945) et al.
- *New History of the Tang* by Ouyang Xiu (1007–72) et al.

These works were written in classical Chinese. For the reader of today, they need to be translated into modern Chinese vernacular with annotations. So, for example, the original *Zhenguan Executive Guide* has 90,000 words, while the modern Chinese version stretches to 450,000.

My grandfather Tang Heng, a classical scholar, taught

me classical Chinese when I was a teenager and gave me a solid grounding in classical prose and poetry as well as calligraphy. I also learned to compose classical verse, which deepened my understanding of classical Chinese. This knowledge stood me in good stead when I carried out research on Tang Taizong. *The Ruler's Guide* has distilled, condensed, and reorganized the original texts in the hope that the wisdom of Tang Taizong might be more accessible to modern Western readers.

The Romanization of Chinese names presents some difficulty. This book adopts the pinyin system, the official phonetic alphabet in China, but some proper names, such as Confucius, Lao Tzu, and Sun Tzu, are spelled in their traditional ways according to the Wade-Giles system because Western readers are already familiar with them.

Dynasties in Chinese History

Xia ca. 2070–1600 BC
Shang ca. 1600–1046 BC
Zhou ca. 1046–256 BC

    Spring and Autumn 770–476 BC
    Warring States 475–221 BC

Qin 221–206 BC
Han 206 BC–AD 220
Three Kingdoms 220–280

    Wei 220–265
    Shu 221–263
    Wu 222–280

Jin 265–420
Northern and Southern 420–589
Sui 581–618
Tang 618–907
Five Dynasties 907–960
Song 960–1279
Yuan 1279–1368
Ming 1368–1644
Qing 1644–1911

Acknowledgments

I am lucky to have a fabulous editor, Rick Horgan, whose inspiring—and inspired—guidance has helped me fashion *The Ruler's Guide* into its current form. I greatly appreciate his cross-cultural insight and global vision as well as his passion for details. I'm much obliged to Jaya Miceli, Kyle Kabel, and Jeff Ward for gracing my book with a handsome cover, elegant interior design, and an excellent map, and to Dan Cuddy for carefully supervising the production process. I would like to thank the entire staff at Scribner for their support and hard work.

I'm heartily grateful to my agent, Nicholas Ellison, for his faith and enthusiasm. I'm deeply indebted to Professor Constance Yang and Audrey Sasaki, who read my earlier drafts and gave me invaluable suggestions. I owe special thanks to Susan Converse Winslow, who read the entire manuscript carefully. Her wise and often-sought counsel has brightened these pages.

My grandfathers and grandmothers taught me to cherish Chinese classics. Their loving memory inspired me to write this book. Both my parents are teachers. In my childhood, they fostered in me a habit of reading and, decades later, as I embarked on this project, gave me their steadfast support. I dedicate this book to them.